D0688024

5816

finger frolics

PP PARTNER PRESS
Box 124
Livonia, Michigan 48152

Sixth Printing, July 1980

ISBN: 0-933212-09-7

Compiled by:

Liz Cromwell, B.A. Elementary Education
M.A. Elementary Education
Certification in Special Education

Dixie Hibner, B.S. Elementary Education
M.A. Elementary Education

Illustrated by:

Sue Yagiela Williams

Edited by:

John R. Faitel

Distributed by Gryphon House
3706 Otis Street
P. O. Box 217
Mt. Rainer, Maryland 20822

INTRODUCTION

Teachers of young children have long been aware of the advantages of play to help a child experience life situations. Fingerplays, a dramatic presentation, using fingers and hands while a verse is being recited, are one method that helps to give a child this experience.

Fingerplays:

1. Help develop language skills
2. Augment general education
3. Teach concepts
3. Can introduce a lesson or unit
5. Reinforce experiences
6. Help develop fine motor skills
7. Increase attention span
8. Increase auditory memory
9. Promote enjoyment in prose and poetry
10. Provide a warm and relaxed atmosphere as a pre-reading environment

The intent of this book is to share a variety of fingerplays that have been used successfully by teachers, parents and others working and playing with children. Fingerplays are very effective when used in conjunction with other early childhood activities. They should be used often but for short periods of time. Favorite fingerplays can be used frequently and new ones introduced gradually.

Have fun with fingerplays!

TABLE OF CONTENTS

SELF CONCEPT

Thumbkin

Where is thumbkin?
Where is thumbkin? (Hide hands behind back)
Here I am (Bring out one hand)
Here I am (Bring out the other)
How are you today, sir? (Nod one thumb)
Very well, I thank you. (Nod the other thumb)
Run away, run away. (Hide thumbs again behind back)

(Repeat using "Pointer", "Tall Man", "Ring Man", and "Pinkie" instead of Thumbkin)

Thumb Man Sings and Dances

Thumb man says he'll dance. (Thumbs up and nod one)
Thumb man says he'll sing. (Nod other thumb)
Dance and sing my merry little thing.
Thumb man says he'll dance and sing.
Pointer says he'll dance, etc.
Tall Man says he'll dance, etc.
Ring man says he'll dance, etc.
Pinkie says he'll dance, etc.

Ten Little Fingers

I have ten little fingers and they all belong to me. (Hands upright)
I can make them do things, would you like to see?
I can shut them up tight; (Shut them up into fists)
Or open them wide. (Open them wide)
I can put them together, or make them all hide. (Close fists together)
I can make them jump high. (Swing hands above head)
I can make them go low. (Swing hands down low)
I can fold them up quietly and hold them just so. (Place in lap)

Head and Shoulder

My hands upon my head I place
Upon my shoulder, upon my face;
At my waist and by my side
And then behind me they will hide.
Then I raise them way up high
And let my fingers swiftly fly;
Then clap, one–two–three
And see how quiet they can be?

Very, Very Tall

I'm very, very tall (Stand on tip toes, arms up)
I'm very, very small (Stoop)
Sometimes I'm tall. (Tiptoes, arms up)
Sometimes I'm small. (Stoop)
Guess what I am now. (May either stoop or stretch)

My Fingers

I stretch my fingers away up high, (Lift fingers and stretch)
Until they almost reach the sky.
I lay them in my lap, you see, (Fold hands in lap)
Where they're as quiet as can be!

Stretch Up High

Stretch up high,
Stretch down low,
Raise your arms
And away we go.

Make a circle in the air,
Sweep your arm around,
Now the other – do the same
And jump up off the ground.

We like to bend,
We like to stretch,
We make our muscles strong.
Bend, stretch
Bend, stretch
All the whole day long.

First I bend my knees,
Then I stand up tall.
Down, up, down, up
Like a rubber ball.
First I'm short,
Then I'm tall.

Touch

Touch your nose,
Touch your chin.
That's the way this game begins.
Touch your eyes,
Touch your knees,
Now pretend you're going to sneeze.
Touch your hair,
Touch one ear,
Touch your two red lips right here.
Touch your elbows
Where they bend
That's the way this touch game ends.

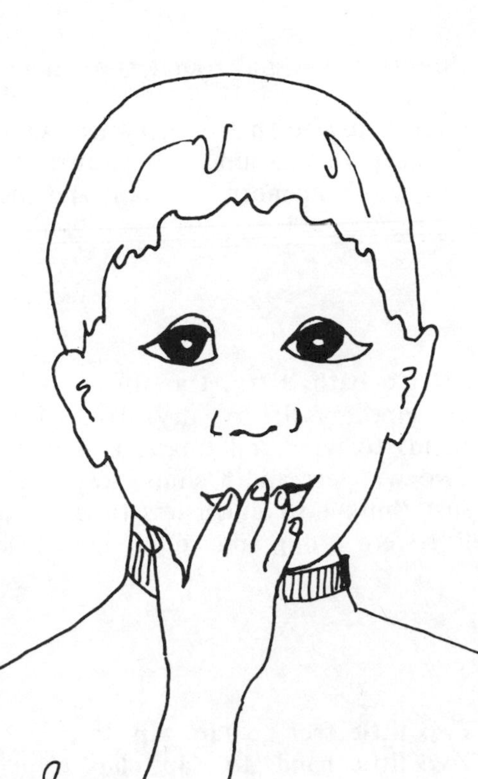

Right and Left

With my left hand, I brush my suit.
With my right hand, I do a salute.
With my left hand, I paint the floor.
With my right hand, I shut the door.

Going to Bed

Climbing, climbing up the stairs,
It's time to go to bed.
I'll thump my fluffy pillow,
Fold back my mother's spread;
I'll brush my teeth and wash my hands,
Turn out my bedside light,
And whisper as I tuck in bed
"God keep me through the night."

This Is the Way We . . .

(Tune: Mulberry Bush
Play as action suggests)

This is the way we wash our hands, etc.
This is the way we comb our hair, etc.
This is the way we brush our teeth, etc.
This is the way we shine our shoes, etc.
This is the way we go to school, etc.

Dirty Hands

Dirty hands are such a fright
See, I washed mine clean and white! (Hold hands out, palms up)
Mother says it is quite right
To wash them morning, noon and night.

Brushing Teeth

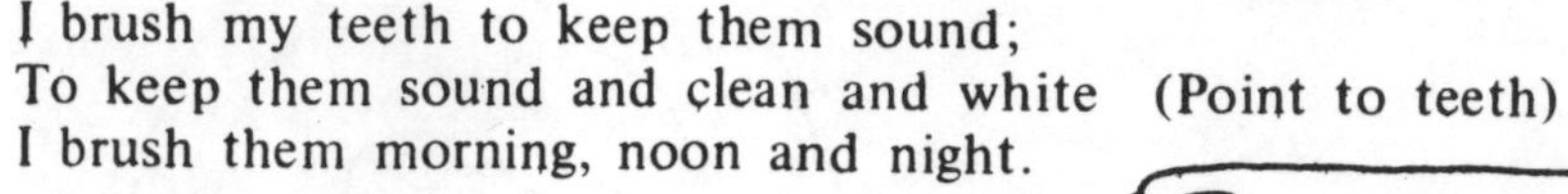

Up and down and round and round (Move right pointer up and down, and round before mouth)
I brush my teeth to keep them sound;
To keep them sound and clean and white (Point to teeth)
I brush them morning, noon and night.

Bath Time

After a bath, I try, try, try
To wipe myself dry, dry, dry. (Rub upper arms with hands)
Hands to wipe and fingers and toes, (Hold hands out, palms up, then point to toes)
Two wet legs and a shiny nose, (Hands on thighs, then point to nose)
Just think how much less time I'd take
If I were a dog and could shake, shake, shake. (Shake body)

Two Little Feet

Two little feet go tap, tap, tap.
Two little hands to clap, clap, clap.
One little leap up from the chair,
Two little arms go up in the air.
Two little hands to thump, thump, thump.
Two little feet go jump, jump, jump.
One little body goes round and round.
One little child sits quietly down.

East and West

This is EAST, and this is WEST. (Face east, then west)
Soon I'll learn to say the rest.
This is HIGH and this is LOW, (Arms over head, then at side)
Only to see how much I know.
This is NARROW, and this is WIDE. (Indicate narrow and wide with hands)
See how much I know beside.
DOWN is where my feet you see, (Point to feet)
UP is where my head should be. (Hand on head)
Here is my nose, and there my eyes. (Point to nose and eyes)
Don't you think I'm getting wise?
Now my eyes will OPEN keep (Open eyes wide)
I SHUT them when I go to sleep. (Shut eyes, lay head on hands)

Going to Bed

This little boy (girl) is going to bed (Lay pointer in palm)
Down on the pillow he lays his head (Thumb acts as pillow)
Covers himself with the blankets so tight (Wrap fingers around "Boy")
And this is the way he sleeps all night. (Close eyes)
Morning comes, and he opens his eyes (Open eyes)
Throws back the covers, and up he flies (Open fingers)
Soon he is up and dressed and away (Pointer stands straight)
Ready for school and ready for play.

Sleepy Head

They call me Little Sleepy Head (Point to head)
I yawn at work, I yawn at play.
I yawn and yawn and yawn all day:
Then, I take my sleepy yawns to bed (Close eyes, lay head on hands)
That's why tney call me sleepy head. (Point to head)

Right Hand

This is my right hand; I raise it up high,
This is my left hand; I'll touch the sky,
Right hand, left hand, roll them around.
Left hand, right hand, pound, pound, pound.

Warm Hands

Warm hands warm. (Rub palms together)
Do you know how?
If you want to warm your hands
Blow your hands now.

Wink – Wink

Make one eye go wink, wink, wink; (Wink one eye)
Make two eyes go blink, blink, blink. (Blink both eyes)
Make two fingers stand just so; (Hold up two fingers)
Then ten fingers in a row. (Hold up ten fingers)
Front and back your head will rock! (Rock head back and forth)
Then your fists will knock, knock, knock. (Thump fists together)
Stretch and make a yawn so wide; (Children stretch and yawn)
Drop your arms down to your sides. (Let arms fall)
Close your eyes and help me say (Close eyes)
Our very quiet sound today.
Sh...........Sh...........shhhhhhhhhhhhhh!

I Wiggle

I wiggle my fingers, (Wiggle fingers)
I wiggle my toes, (Wiggle toes)
I wiggle my shoulders, (Wiggle shoulders)
I wiggle my nose. (Wiggle nose)
Now no more wiggles are left in me.
So I will be still as still can be.

Open, Shut Them

Open, shut them; open, shut them;
Give them a clap.
Open, shut them; open, shut them;
Lay them in your lap.
Creep them, creep them slowly upward
To your rosy cheeks.
Open wide your shiny eyes
And through your fingers peek.
Open, shut them; open, shut them;
To your shoulders fly.
Let them, like the little birdies,
Flutter to the sky.
Falling, falling, slowly falling,
Nearly to the ground,
Quickly raising all your fingers,
Twirling them around.
Open, shut them; open, shut them;
Give them a clap.
Open, shut them; open, shut them;
Lay them in your lap.

Stretch, Stretch

Stretch, stretch away up high; (Reach arms upward)
On your tiptoes, reach the sky. (Stand on tiptoes and reach)
See the bluebirds flying high. (Wave hands)
Now bend down and touch your toes; (Bend to touch toes)
Now sway as the North Wind blows. (Move body back and forth)
Waddle as the gander goes! (Walk in waddling motion back to seats)

Ready to Listen

Let your hands go clap, clap, clap; (Clap hands three times)
Let your fingers snap, snap, snap; (Snap fingers three times)
Let your lips go very round. (Make lips round)
But do not make a sound.
Fold your hands and close each eye; (Follow action indicated)
Take a breath . . . . and softly sigh: (Follow action indicated)
Ah - - - - - - - - - - - - - - - - - - -

Readiness

Close your eyes, head drop down,
Face is smooth, not a frown;
Roll to left; head is a ball;
Roll right; now sit tall!
Lift your chin; look at me!
Take deep breaths, one, two, three;
Make big smiles; hands in lap;
Make believe you've had a nap.
Now you've rested from your play.
Try to work again today!

Still Time

I've just come in from playing;
I'm as tired as I can be.
I'll cross my legs
And fold my hands
And close my eyes so I can't see.
I will not move my body;
I'll be like Raggedy Ann;
My head won't move;
My arms won't move;
I'll just be still
Because I can.

Stand Up Tall

Stand up tall; (Children stand)
Hands in the air; (Raise hands)
Clap your hands; (Clap three times as words are said)
Make a frown; (Children knit brows)
Smile and smile, (Children smile)
And flop like a clown! (Children relax with arms dangling)

Hand On Myself

Hand on myself (Point to head)
What is this here?
This is my new noggin, my mother dear.

New noggin, new noggin,
Nick, nick, nick new.
That's what I learned in the school

Hand on myself (Point to eye)
What is this here?
This is my eye winker, my mother dear.

Eye winker, new noggin
Nick, nick, nick new
That's what I learned in the school

Hand on myself (Point to nose)
What is this here?
This is my nose blower, my mother dear.

Nose blower, eye winker, new noggin
Nick, nick, nick new
That's what I learned in the school

Hand on myself . . . .
(Point to mouth eater and repeat.
Next, chin chopper and bread basket.)

HOME

This Is My Family

This is my mother (Thumb)
This is my father (Pointer Finger)
This is my brother tall (Middle finger)
This is my sister (Ring finger)
This is the baby (Little finger)
Oh, how we love them all. (Clap left hand over all fingers just indicated)

My Whole Family

This is the mother good and dear (Thumb)
This is the father standing near (Pointer finger)
This is the boy who plays with a ball (Middle finger)
This is the girl who plays with her doll (Ring finger)
This is the baby, the pet of all (Little finger)
See the whole family, big and small! (Show all five fingers)

Knives and Forks

Here are mother's knives and forks (Interlock fingers, palms up)
This is the father's table (Keep fingers interlocked and turn palms down)
This is sister's looking glass (Make peak of two pointers)
And this is the baby's cradle. (Add peak of little fingers and rock)

Grandma

These are Grandma's glasses (Make circles around eyes with pointer and thumb)
This is Grandma's cap (Place hands on head)
This is the way she folds her hands (Fold hands)
And lays them in her lap. (Lay in lap)

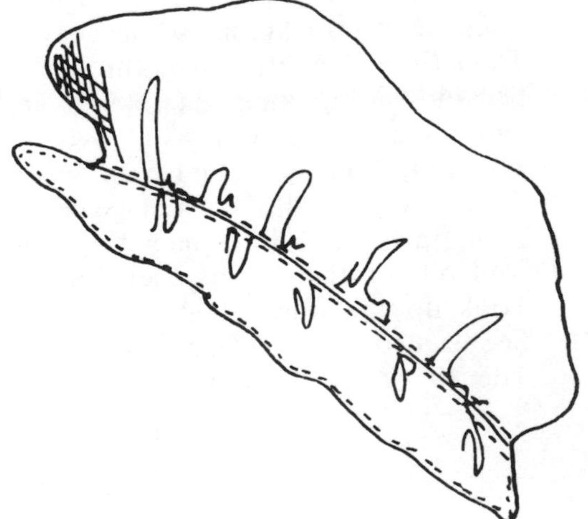

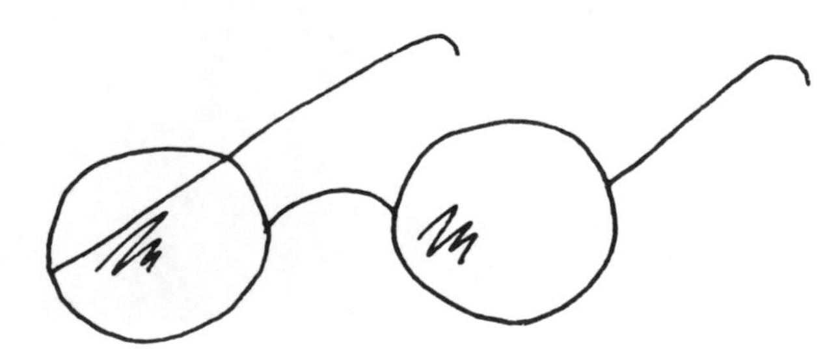

Baby

Here's a ball for baby (Make circle with thumb and pointer)
Big and soft and round.
Here is the baby's hammer, (Make hammer with fist)
Oh, how he can pound!
Here is baby's music, (Hold up hands facing each other)
Clapping, clapping, so, (Clap hands)
Here are baby's soldiers (Hold fingers upright)
Standing in a row.
Here is baby's trumpet, Toot-too, too-too, too, (Two fists, one atop the other before mouth)
Here's the way that baby
Plays at peek-a-boo. (Fingers of both hands spread before eyes)
Here's a big umbrella (Bring fingertips together in peak over head)
To keep the baby dry.
Here is baby's cradle. (Make peak of pointers and little fingers and rock)
Rock a baby bye.

A Good House

This is the roof of the house so good (Make roof with hands)
These are the walls that are made of wood (Hands straight, palms parallel)
These are the windows that let in the light (Thumbs and forefingers form window)
This is the door that shuts so tight (Hands straight side by side)
This is the chimney so straight and tall (Arms up straight)
Oh! What a good house for one and all. (Arms at angle for roof)

Funny Little Man

There's a funny little man (thumb) in a funny little house (Wrap fingers around "man")
And right across the way, there's another funny little man in another funny little house. (Other hand)
And they play hide and seek all day.
One funny little man through his window peeps (Thumb between fingers)
Sees no one looking, then softly creeps (Thumb crawls out)
Out his door, he comes so slow
Looks up and down and high and low (Thumb up and down)
Then back into his house he goes (Thumb back in fist)
Then the other little man through his window peeps (Thumb between fingers)
Sees no one looking, then softly creeps (Thumb crawls out)
Out his door, he comes so slow
Looks up and down and high and low (Thumb up and down)
Then back into his house he goes (Thumb back in fist)
Sometimes these little men forget to peep
And out of their doors they softly creep (Both thumbs)
Look up and down, high and low
See each other and laugh "Ho ho!"
Then back into their houses they go.

My Family

Here is my pretty mother; (Point to pointer finger)
Here is my father tall; (Point to middle finger)
Here is my older brother, (Point to ring finger)
And that isn't all;
Here is my baby brother, (Point to little finger)
As small as small can be;
Who is this other person? (Point to thumb)
Why, of course, it's ME!
1, 2, 3, 4, 5, you see, (Touch each finger as you count)
Make a very nice family!

See My Family

See my family. See them all (Hold up five fingers)
Some are short, (Hold up thumb)
And some are tall. (Hold up middle finger)

Let's shake hands. "How do you do?" (Clasp hands and shake)
See them bow. "How are you?" (Bend fingers)
Father, (Hold up middle finger)
Mother, (Hold up pointer finger)
Sister, (Hold up ring finger)
Brother, (Hold up thumb)
And me, (Hold up little finger)
All polite to one another.

SEASONS

Autumn

Ten Red Apples

Ten red apples grow on a tree (Both hands high)
Five for you and five for me (Dangle one hand and then the other)
Let us shake the tree just so (Shake body)
And ten red apples will fall below (Hands fall)
1, 2, 3, 4, 5, 6, 7, 8, 9, 10 (Count each finger)

Ten Rosy Apples

Ten rosy apples high in a tree (Arms above head, fingers separated)
Safely hiding where no one can see.
When the wind comes rocking to and fro. (Arms sway above head)
Ten rosy apples to the ground must go. ("Apples tumble down to the floor)

In the Apple Tree

Away up high in an apple tree (Point up)
Two red apples smiled at me (Form circles with fingers)
I shook that tree as hard as I could (Shake tree)
Down came the apples and m-m-m m-m they were good. (Rub stomach)

If I Were an Apple

If I were an apple
And grew on a tree (Fingertips and thumbs touch overhead to form apple)
I think I'd drop down
On a nice boy like me.
I wouldn't stay there
Giving nobody joy --
I'd fall down at once ("Apple" falls down into lap)
And say, "Eat me, my boy."

When the Leaves Are on the Ground

When the leaves are on the ground, (Point to floor)
Instead of on the trees, (Hands clasped over head)
I like to make a great big pile of them
Way up to my knees. (Hands on knees)
I like to run and jump in them (Jump once)
And kick them all around. (Kicking motion with foot)
I like the prickly feel of them
And the crickly, crackly, sound. (Click fingernails)

Fall

The leaves are green, the nuts are brown, (Raise arms sideward, wiggle fingers, make circles for nuts)
They hang so high they will never fall down, (Stretch arms)
Leave them alone till the bright fall weather (Move hands as if wind blows softly)
And then they will all come down together. (Bring arms down to side quickly)

Leaves Are Floating Down

Leaves are floating softly down; (Flutter fingers)
They make a carpet on the ground
Then, swish! The wind comes whirling by (Bring hand around rapidly)
And sends them dancing to the sky. (Flutter fingers upward)

Winter

Winter Is Coming

Into their hives the busy bees crawl. (Make ten fingers walk)
Into the ant hills go ants one and all. (Continue same motion)
The brown caterpillars have hidden their heads. (Put one fist under opposite arm)
They spin silk cocoons for their snug little beds. (Motion of spinning)
The squirrels have gone into their holes in the tree. (Move hands behind back)
The birds' nests are empty. No birds do we see. (Show palms)
The elves have all gone for the winter, we know.
There isn't a person who knows where they go. (Fold hands)

Mrs. Peck Pigeon

Mrs. Peck Pigeon
Is pecking for bread,
Bob–bob–bob (Bob head up and down)
Goes her little round head.
Tame as a pussy cat
In the street.
Step, step, step (Take three steps)
Go her little red feet (Point to feet)
Mrs. Peck Pigeon
Goes pecking for bread. (Bob head up and down

Susie's Galoshes

Susie's galoshes make splishes and sploshes (Slide feet along floor)
And slooshes and sloshes
As Susie steps slowly
Along in the slush.
They stamp and they stamp (Stamp twice)
On the ice and concrete.
They get stuck in the mush and the mud.
But Susie likes best to hear
The slippery slush, (Slide feet along floor)
As it slooshes and sloshes
And splishes and sploshes
All around her galoshes.

Boots

Boots never seem to fit. (Hands on hips, shake head)
They're either too big, (Spread arms wide to show size)
And slippy and sloppy,
Or else too small, (Hands together to show size)
And sticky and stucky!
Can't get them off, (Try to pull boots off)
Whether I stand on one leg (Stand on one leg)
Or whether I sit. (Sit down)
Boots never seem to fit! (Hands on hips, shake head)

Little Pig

(With pointer finger of right hand, touch fingers and thumb of left hand – starting with little finger:)

This little pig lost his sweater,
This little pig lost her muff.
Said this little pig, "Jack Forst will catch you."
Said this little pig, "Sure enough."
Said this little pig, "Br–r–r–r wee, wee, wee,
This nice warm house is the place for me." (Put thumb in fist)

My Zipper Suit

My zipper suit is bunny brown
The top zips up, (Pretend to zip top up)
The legs zip down. (Pretend to zip leg zippers down)
I wear it every day.
My daddy brought it out from town.
Zip it up, (Pretend to zip top up)
Zip it down, (Pretend to zip leg zippers down)
And hurry out to play.

Burr–rr–rr

Today I wore my snow suit
That goes from heels to throat. (Point to feet, then neck)
It shuts up with a zip, (Pretend to zip up front)
And is much warmer than a coat.

I wore a sweater under that,
And a wooly cap, bright red. (Make cap on head)
It fitted snug upon my ears (Hands on ears)
And covered my whole head! (Circular motion about head)

I wore overshoes with buckles (Point to shoes)
And mittens lined with fur, (Hand out, fingers together)
But just the same, when I went out,
I shivered and said, "Burr–rr–rr." (Shiver, arms close to body)

Jack Frost Paid a Visit

Jack Frost paid me a visit
On a January night;
He painted funny little shapes
On windows, what a sight!
He made a picture of a square, (Children draw square in the air)
And of a circle, too; (Children draw circle)
He made a pointed triangle; (Form triangle with two index fingers and thumbs)
Oh, these were just a few!
There was a curve just like an S. (Make an S in the air)
Some big waves went this way; (Make W movements)
Some humpy shapes looked like an M; (Make M movements)
I saw some tails like a J. (Make one large J)
There were four fence posts standing straight; (Draw 4 straight lines)
I counted them, you see;
And then there were some slanted lines; (Make 3 slanted lines)
I think that there were three.
So many shapes! So many shapes!
Some different; some the same;
I learned them all, and then I found
That some were in my name!

Jack Frost

Jack Frost is a fairy small, (Show smallness with thumb and pointer)
I'm sure he is out today.
He nipped my nose (Point to nose)
And pinched my toes (Point to toes)
When I went out to play.

I am a Snowman

Now I am a snowman (Stand with arms out)
Standing on the lawn.
I melt and melt and melt
And pretty soon I'm gone. (Body slumps and voice fades)

Make a Snowman

Start with a very tiny ball, (Form ball with fingers)
Roll it through the snow. (Push with right hand)
Over and over and over again. (Repeat pushing motion)
Each turn makes it grow.

Now the ball is big and round (Make ball with arms)
Make it broad and tall. (Indicate with arms)
Add a head and then some arms (Motion as if setting them on)
Firm so they won't fall.

Here are buttons for his coat (Pretend to place)
A broom for him to hold. (Pretend to hold a broom)
Let's put a hat upon his head, (Pretend to put hat on own head)
So he won't get cold.

Gather Snow

Gather snow and make a ball. (Hands in ball formation)
Make a snowman round and tall (Indicate with hands)
Coal for buttons, (Pretend to place buttons)
Coal for eyes (Pretend to place eyes)
There he stands and looks so wise, (Stand like a snowman)

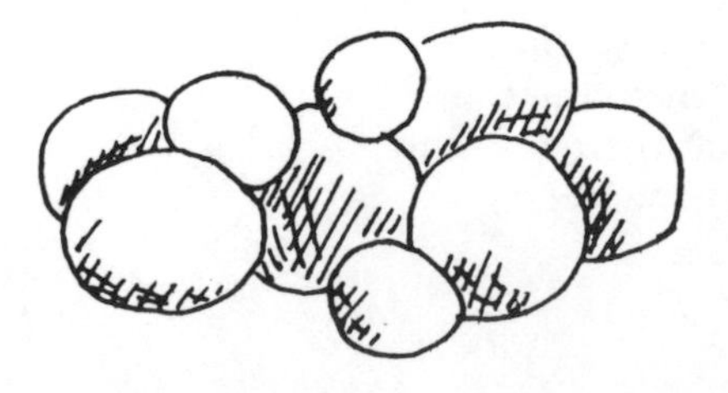

Chubby Little Snowman

A chubby little snowman
Had a carrot nose. (Point to nose)
Along came a bunny
And what do you suppose? (Hold up two fingers on right hand to make a bunny)

That hungry little bunny
Looking for his lunch
Ate that little snowman's nose (Pretend to grab nose)
Nibble, nibble, crunch.

Crickle, Crackle

When it is winter time
I run up the street (Take three running steps)
And I make the ice laugh
With my little feet (Point to the feet)
"Crickle, crackle, crickle (Hold feet up alternatively with each word)
Crrrreet, crreet, crreet."

Once There Was a Snowman

Once there was a snowman (Stand like a snowman)
Who stood outside my door.
He thought he'd like to come inside
And run around the floor. (Run in a small circle)
He thought he'd like to warm himself (Hold hands out before imaginary fire)
By the fireside red.
He thought he'd like to climb upon (Climbing motion)
The big white bed.
So he called to the North Wind
"Help me now, I pray. (Hands together, palm to palm)
I'm completely frozen
Standing here all day." (Huddle arms together)
So the north wind came along
And blew him in the door
And now there's nothing left of him
But a puddle on the floor. (Point to floor)

Snowflakes

Said the first little snowflake (Hold pointer finger up)
As he whirled from the sky,
"I'll light on that red chimney.
It looks nice and high."

Said the second little snowflake, (Hold middle finger up)
"Oh, that is not for me.
I shall feel much safer
In the old apple tree."

Said the third little snowflake, (Hold ring finger up)
"Through the air I'll skim
'Til I light on some boy's shoulder.
Then I'll go to school with him."

I Am a Snowman

I am a snowman, cold and white;
I stand so still through all the night; (Stand up tall)
With a carrot nose, (Point to nose)
And head held high,
And lump of coal to make each eye. (Point to eyes)
I have a muffler made of red, (Indicate neck)
And a stovepipe hat upon my head. (Place hands on top of head)
The sun is coming out! Oh, my! (Make circle for sun)
I think that I am going to cry; (Start sinking to floor)
Yesterday, I was so plump and round;
Now I'm just a river on the ground. (Sink to the floor)

Snowman in our Yard

We made a snowman in our yard,
Jolly and round, and fat. (Hold hands under stomach and jiggle it)
We gave him father's pipe to smoke (Pretend to hold pipe)
And father's battered hat. (Tap top of head)
We tied a scarf around his neck (Pretend to tie scarf)
And in his buttonhole
We stuck a holly spray, (Pretend to put holly in buttonhole)
He had black buttons made of coal (Indicate buttons)
He had black eyes, a turned up nose, (Indicate eyes and nose)
A wide and cheerful grin;
And there he stood in our front yard, (Stand tall)
Inviting company in! (Make motion with hand)

Merry Little Snowflakes

Merry little snowflakes falling through the air; (Fingers raised high and moving rapidly)
Resting on the steeple and the tall trees everywhere; (Make steeple with two pointer fingers and then raise arms for branches)
Covering roofs and fences, capping every post; (Two hands forming roof, then hands clasped)
Covering the hillside where we like to coast. (Make scooping motion like coasting)
Merry little snowflakes do their very best (Fingers raised high and moving rapidly)
To make a soft, white blanket so buds and flowers may rest; (Psalms together at side of face)
But when the bright spring sunshine says it's come to stay, (Make circle of arms for sun)
Then those little snowflakes quickly run away! (Hide hands behind back)

Little Snowman

I made a little snowman with hat and cane complete. (Hold out hand to indicate little snowman)
With shiny buttons on his coat and shoes upon his feet. (Indicate buttons and shoes)
But I know when the sun comes out, my snowman will go away. (Make circle with arms)
So I'll put him in our big deep freeze, and he'll be sure to stay.

Snowman

Roll a snowball large, (Arms make a circle)
Then one of middle size; (Two pointer fingers and two thumbs make a circle)
Roll a snowball small; (One pointer finger and thumb)
Use lumps of coal for eyes. (Point to eyes)
An old hat upon his head, (Place both hands on top of head)
And for his necktie, tie around
His neck a ribbon red. (Motion of tying ribbon)
A corn cob pipe goes in his mouth, (Point to mouth)
Some buttons on his vest; (Point to buttons down front)
Of snowmen, he's the best!

One Little, Two Little, Three Little Snowmen

One little, two little, three little snowmen, (Hold up one finger for each snowman)
Four little, five little, six little snowmen,
Seven little, eight little, nine little snowmen,
Ten little snowmen bright.

Ten little, nine little, eight little snowmen,
Seven little, six little, five little snowmen,
Four little, three little, two little snowmen,
One little snowman bright.

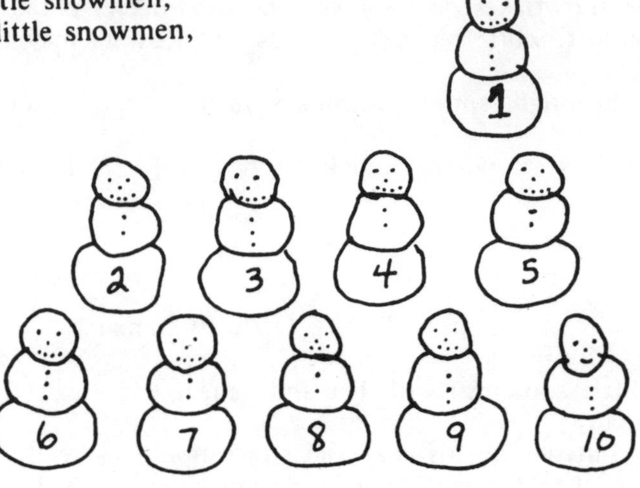

Tune: Mary had a Little Lamb

1. Snow piled up will make a hill, make a hill, make a hill. (Pretend to pile up
   Snow piled up will make a hill for sliding in a yard. snow)

2. We roll it up in great big balls, great big balls, great big balls
   We roll it up in great big balls and pound it 'til it's hard. (Roll hands and then pound one fist on other palm)

3. Though other children call to us, call to us, call to us.
   Though other children call to us to take our sleds outside. (Place hands to mouth)

4. We don't go out but stay right home, stay right home, stay right home.
   We don't go out but stay right home and slide and slide and slide. (Make sliding motion with hand)

Tree in Winter

Outside the door the bare tree stands, (Palms together high overhead)
And catches snowflakes in its hands, (Hold above position but open palms to catch snowflakes)
And holds them well and holds them high
Until a puffing wind comes by. (Resume first position)

Spring

Five Little Robins

Five little robins up in a tree,
Father (Thumb), Mother (Pointer)
And babies three, (Middle, ring and little fingers)
Father caught a worm, (Point to thumb)
Mother caught a bug, (Pointer finger)
This one got the bug, (Middle finger)
This one got the worm, (Ring finger)
This one said, "Now it's my turn". (Little finger)

Ten Little Pigeons

Ten little pigeons sat in a line (Hands stretched up over head)
Up on the barn in the warm sunshine.
Ten little pigeons flew down to the ground. (Flutter fingers down)
And ate the crumbs that were lying around.

My Pigeon House

My pigeon house I open wide (Open fist)
To set my pigeons free (Fingers free)
They fly over fields on every side (Flying)
And then fly back to me. (Fingers return)
And when they return from their merry flight
I close the door, and softly say, "Good-night". (Close fist)

Little Birds

High, high, high, up in the sky (Hold both arms up)
The little birds fly (Make fingers fly)
Down, down, down, in the nest (Bring arms down, fingers resting on lap)
With a wing on the left (Hold up left hand)
With a wing on the right (Hold up right hand)
They sleep and they sleep
All through the night.

Five Little Sparrows

Five little sparrows high in a tree (Hold one hand up)
The first one said, "Whom do I see?" (Point to thumb)
The second one said, "I see the street." (Pointer finger)
The third one said, "And seeds to eat." (Middle finger)
The fourth one said, "The seeds are wheat." (Ring finger)
The fifth one said, "Tweet, tweet, tweet." (Little finger)

Houses

Here is a nest for the robin; (Cup both hands)
Here is a hive for the bee; (Fists together)
Here is a hole for the bunny; (Finger and thumb form circle)
And here is a house for ME! (Fingertips together make roof)

The Woodpecker

The woodpecker pecked out a little round hole (Tap left palm with right pointer)
And made him a house in the telephone pole.
One day as I watched he poked out his head. (Poke out head)
He had on a hood and a collar of red. (Point to head and neck)
When the streams of rain pour out of the sky,
And the flashes of lightening go streaking by
And the big, big wheels of thunder roll, (Roll arms)
He can snuggle back in his telephone pole.

Two Little Birds

Here are two tall telegraph poles (Hold up pointer fingers)
And between them a wire is strung (Join thumbs at tops)
Two little birds are flying by (Wiggle middle fingers)
They hopped on the wire and swung. (Middle fingers on thumbs)
To and fro, to and fro (Swing hands back and forth
They hopped on the wire and swung.

Little Birdie

What does little birdie say
In her nest at peek of day?
"Let me fly," says little birdie, (Wiggle thumb)
"Mother, let me fly away."
Birdie, rest a little longer, (Wiggle other thumb)
'Til your little wings are stronger."
So she rests a little longer.
Then she flies away. (First thumb fly away)

My Kite

The winds of March begin to blow,
And it is time for kites, you know.
Here's the way I make my kite;
Watch and help me do it right.
I cross two sticks, so thin and long, (Cross pointer fingers)
Tied together good and strong; (Motion of tying)
And across the middle to make it bend;
I measure and cut the paper gay, (Motion of measuring and cutting)
And paste along the edge this way; (Motion of pasting)
A ball of string to hold my kite, (Form a circle with fingers)
When it sails almost out of sight;
And here's my kite all ready to go! (Hands outstretched)
Please, March Wind, begin to blow!

The Wind

The wind came out to play one day.
He swept the clouds out of his way; (Make sweeping motion)
He blew the leaves and away they flew. (Make fluttering motions with fingers)

The trees bent low and their branches did too. (Lift arms and lower them)
The wind blew the great big ships at sea; (Repeat sweeping motions)
The wind blew the kite away from me.

Roly–Poly Caterpillar

Roly–poly caterpillar
Into a corner crept,
Spun around himself a blanket (Spin around)
Then for a long time slept. (Place head on folded hands)
Roly–poly caterpillar
Wakening by and by –– (Stretch)
Found himself with beautiful wings
Changed to a butterfly. (Flutter arms like wings)

Butterfly

Bright colored butterfly, (Place hands back to back and wiggle fingers)
Looking for honey,
Spread your wings and fly away,
While it's sunny.

Fuzzy Little Caterpillar

Fuzzy little caterpillar
Crawling, crawling on the ground (Move hand forward, wiggle thumb)
Fuzzy little caterpillar
Nowhere to be found,
Though we've looked and looked
And hunted everywhere around.

Eensy, Weensy Spider

An eensy, weensy spider (Opposite thumbs and pointer fingers)
Climbed up the water-spout, (Climb up each other)
Down came the rain
And washed the spider out. (Hands sweep down)
Out came the sunshine (Arms form circle overhead)
And dried up all the rain (Arms sweep upward)
And the eensy, weensy spider
Climbed up the spout again. (As above)

Here Is the Bee Hive

Here is the bee-hive. Where are the bees? (Make fist)
They're hiding away so nobody sees,
Soon they'll come creeping out of their hive,
One, two, three, four, five. Buzz–z–z–z–z–z–z–z. (Draw fingers out of fist on each count)

Tadpoles

Dive, little tadpole, one; (Hold up one finger)
Dive, little tadpole, two (Hold up two fingers)
Swim, little tadpoles,
Oh, oh, oh. (Clap three times)
Or I will catch YOU! (Point)

Sleepy Caterpillars

"Let's go to sleep," the little caterpillars said, (Wiggle fingers)
As they tucked themselves into their beds. (Make fists)
They will awaken by and by,
And each one will be a lovely butterfly. (Open hand, one finger at a time)

Five Little May Baskets

Five little May baskets waiting by the door; (Hold up five fingers)
One will go to Mrs. Smith, then there will be four. (Bend down one finger)
Four little May baskets, pretty as can be;
One will go to Mrs. Brown, then there will be three. (Bend down one finger)
Three little May baskets, one is pink and blue;
It will go to Mr. Jones, then there will be two. (Bend down one finger)
Two little May baskets yellow as the sun;
One will go to Mr. Black, then there will be one. (Bend one finger down)
One little May basket; oh, it's sure to go
To my own mother, who's the nicest one I know. (Cup hands to form basket)

Flowers

Flowers tall, (Let tall fingers stand up)
Flowers small, (Let small fingers and thumb stand up)
Count them one by one,
Blowing with the breezes
In the springtime sun!
1, 2, 3, 4, 5 (Touch as you count)

Rose

I like to pretend that I am a rose (Cup hands)
That grows and grows and grows and grows. (Open hands gradually)
My hands are a rosebud closed up tight, (Close hands)
With not a tiny speck of light,
Then slowly the petals open for me. (Let hands come apart gradually)
And here is a full-grown rose, you see!

Ten Little Leaf Buds

Ten little leaf buds growing on a tree (Fingers are buds)
Curled up as tightly as can be (Curl fingers up into fists)
See them keeping snug and warm,
During the winters cold and storm. (Snuggle fist under fist)
Now along comes windy March,
With his breath now soft, now harsh.
First he swings them roughly so (Swing fists back and forth)
Then more gently to and fro (Swing tenderly)
'Til the raindrops from the skies (Stretch arms high, bring down to floor, tapping fingers as rain)
Falling pitter, patter-wise (Repeat previous action)
Open wide the leaf bud's eyes. (Arms outstretched, open fists and spread fingers at the word "eyes".)

Little Brown Seed

I'm a little brown seed in the ground
Rolled up in a tiny ball; (Sitting on heels, on the floor, drop head over knees)
I'll wait for the rain and sunshine; (In the same position, place arms over head and wiggle fingers downward for rain; then place both hands in large circle over head, for sun)
To make me big and tall. (Stand straight stretching arms over head)

Seeds

I work in my garden,
Plant seeds in a row;
The rain and the sunshine (Flutter fingers, make circle with arms)
Will help them to grow.
Sometimes when the weather
Is too dry and hot,
I sprinkle the earth
With my watering pot. (Make fist of four fingers, thumb pointing down)
The roots pushing downward, (Place one hand on the other wrist, fingers on other hand spread apart and pointing down)
The stems pushing up
My blossoms have opened, (Hands out, palms up with fingers curling up in cup-like manner)
Rose, pink, buttercup.

My Garden

This is my garden; (Extend one hand forward, palm up)
I'll rake it with care, (Make raking motion on palm with three fingers of other hand)
And then some flower seeds (Planting motion)
I'll plant in there.
The sun will shine (Make circle with hands)
And the rain will fall, (Let fingers flutter down to lap)
And my garden will blossom (Cup hands together; extend upward slowly)
And grow straight and tall.

My Little Garden

In my little garden bed (Extend one hand, palm up)
Raked so nicely over (Use three fingers for rake)
First the tiny seeds I plant
Then with soft earth cover, (Use planting and covering motion)
Shining down, the great round sun (Circle with arms)
Smiles upon it often;
Little raindrops, pattering down, (Flutter fingers)
Help the seeds to soften.
Then the little plant awakes --
Down the roots go creeping, (Fingers downward)
Up it lifts its little head (Fingers held close together pointing upward)
Through the brown earth peeping.
High and higher still it grows. (Raise arms, fingers still cupped)
Through the summer hours,
Till some happy day the buds
Open into flowers. (Spread fingers)

Mister Carrot

Nice Mister Carrot
Makes curly hair, (Hand on head)
His head grows underneath the ground (Bob head)
His feet up in the air. (Raise feet)
And early in the morning
I find him in his bed (Close eyes, lay head on hands)
And give his feet a great big pull (Stretch legs out)
And out comes his head!

Green Leaf

Here's a green leaf, (Show hand)
And here's a green leaf, (Show other hand)
That you see, makes two.
Here is a bud (Cup hands together)
That makes a flower;
Watch it bloom for you! (Open cupped hands gradually)

Yellow Daffodil

Here is a yellow daffodil
That nods from left to right; (Raise arm and weave back and forth)
Here are the leaves so soft and green
That guard it through the night. (Hold up ten fingers, then bring them together and fold hands)

Five Little Flowers

Five little flowers
Standing in the sun! (Hold up five fingers)
See their heads nodding,
Bowing, one by one. (Bend fingers several times)
Down, down, down
Comes the gentle rain, (Raise hands, wiggle fingers, and lower arms to simulate rain)
And the five little flowers
Lift up their heads again! (Hold up five fingers)

Purple Violets

One purple violet in our garden grew; (Hold up one finger)
Up popped another, and that made two. (Hold up two fingers)
Two purple violets were all that I could see;
But Billy found another, and that made three. (Hold up three fingers)
Three purple violets – if I could find one more,
I'd make a wreath for Mother, and that would make four. (Hold up four fingers)
Four purple violets – sure as you're alive!
Why, here is another! And now there are five! (Hold up five fingers)

Raindrops

Raindrops, raindrops!
Falling all around. (Move fingers to imitate falling rain)
Pitter-patter on the rooftops, (Tap softly on desk or floor)
Pitter-patter on the ground.
Here is my umbrella;
It will keep me dry. (Hands over head)
When I go walking in the rain,
I hold it up so high. (Raise hands in air)

Pitter-patter, raindrops!
Falling from the sky; (Wiggle fingers to imitate falling rain)
Here is my umbrella
To keep me safe and dry! (Hands over head)
When the rain is over,
And the sun begins to glow, (Make a large circle with arms)
Little flowers start to bud, (Cup two hands together)
And grow, and grow, and grow!

Pitter, Patter

Oh! Where do you come from,
You little drops of rain,
Pitter, patter, pitter, patter (Tap fingers on table or floor)
Down the window pane?

Tell me, little raindrops,
Is that the way you play,
Pitter, patter, pitter, patter (Tap fingers as before)
All the rainy day.

Rain

The storm came up so very quick
It couldn't have been quicker
I should have brought my hat along. (Place flat palm on top of head)
I should have brought my slicker, (Indicate slicker)
My hair is wet, my feet are wet, (Point to head and feet)
I couldn't be much wetter,
I fell into a river once
But this is even wetter.

Storm

Black clouds are giants hurrying (Make circle with arms and move quickly)
Across the field of the sky,
And they slip out bolts of lightening
As they go racing by.
When they meet each other
They shake hands and thunder (Pretend to shake hands)
How do you do! How do you do!
HOW DO YOU DO!

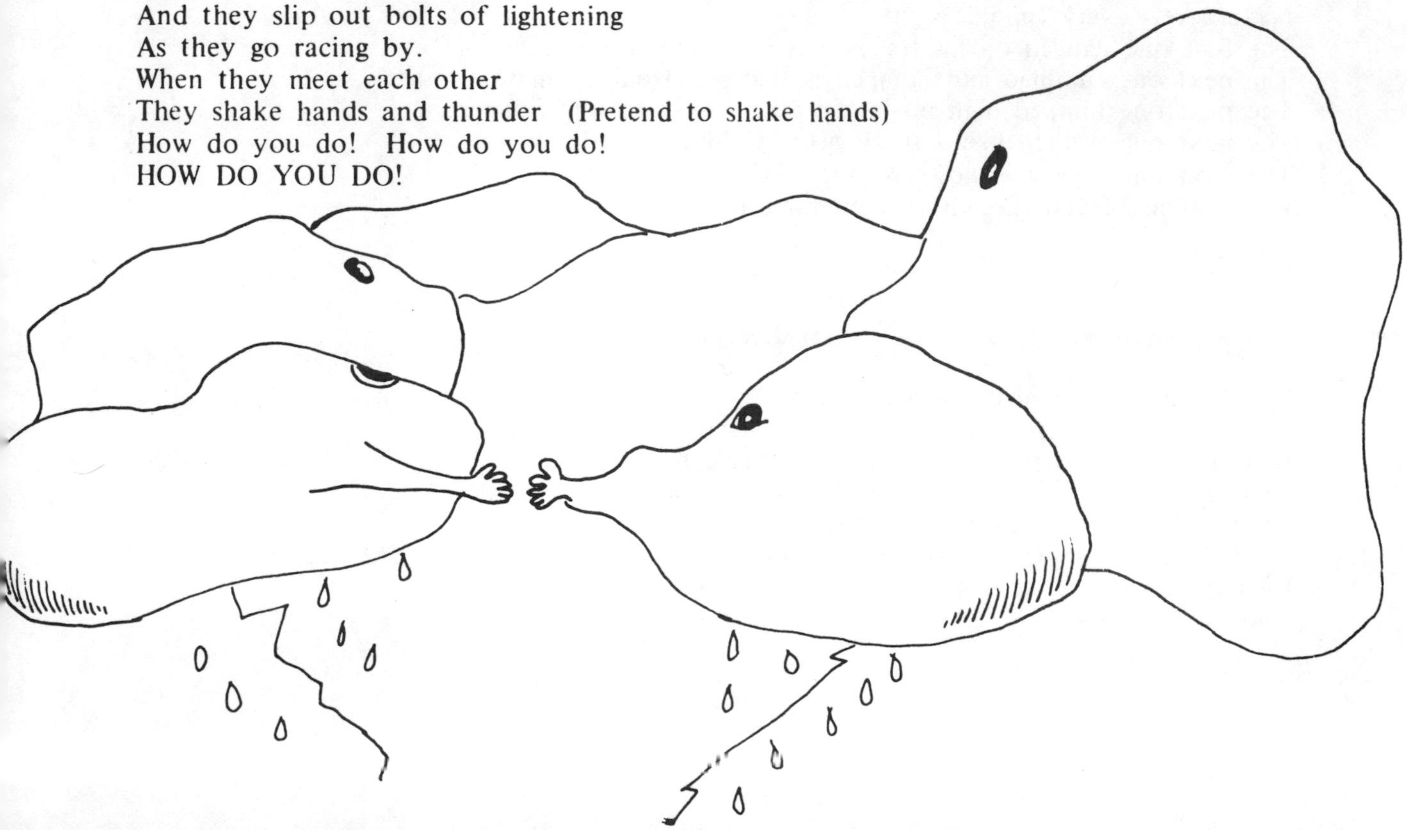

HOLIDAYS

Halloween

Black Cat

A big black cat with eyes so green (Point to eyes)
Went out on the night of Halloween.
He saw a witch. (Bring fingertips together in peak over head)
He saw an owl. (Bring index finger and thumb of both hands together and place before eyes)
And then he began to "Meow, Meow,"

Five Little Ghosts

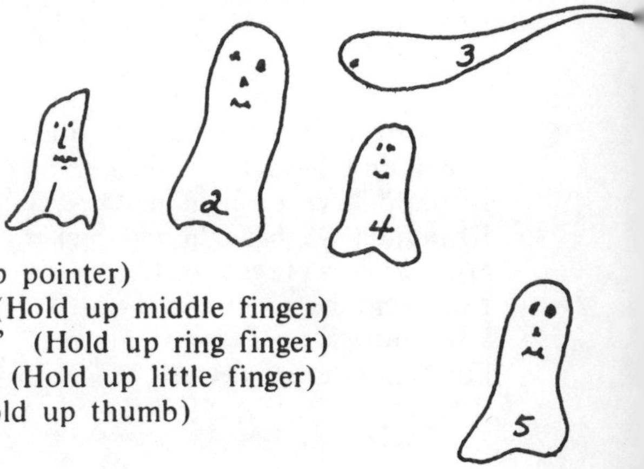

Five little ghosts dressed all in white
Were scaring each other on Halloween night.
"Boo!" said the first one, "I'll catch you!" (Hold up pointer)
"Wooo" said the second, "I don't care if you do!" (Hold up middle finger)
The third ghost said, "You can't run away from me." (Hold up ring finger)
And the fourth one said, "I'll scare everyone I see." (Hold up little finger)
Then the last one said, "It's time to disappear." (Hold up thumb)
See you at Halloween time next year!"

Five Little Goblins

Five little goblins on a Halloween night
Made a very, very spookie sight.
The first one danced on his tippy-tip-toes; (Hold up pointer)
The next one tumbled and bumped his nose; (Hold up middle finger)
The next one jumped high up in the air; (Hold up ring finger)
The next one walked like a fuzzy bear; (Hold up little finger)
The next one sang a Halloween song. (Hold up thumb)
Five goblins played the whole night long!

Wide-eyed Owl

Here's a wide-eyed owl. (Bring pointer finger and thumb of both hands together and place before eyes)
With a pointed nose (Make a peak with two forefingers and place before nose)
And claws for toes. (Hands arched before chest fingers curled)
He lives high in a tree (Hands clasped high above head)
When he looks at you (Index finger and thumb of both hands together before eyes)
He flaps his wings (Bend elbows, flap hands)
And says, "Whoo, whoo–o–o". (Make "whoo" sound)

Owl

An owl sat on the branch of a tree (Owl is right forefinger. The branch is left)
And he was quiet as quiet could be.
'Twas night and his eyes were open like this (Circle eyes with thumb and forefinger)
And he looked all around; not a thing did he miss (Look about)
Some brownies climbed up the trunk of the tree (Put owl back on perch)
And sat on a branch as quiet as he. (Move middle, ring and little fingers of right hand next to owl)
Said the wise old owl, "To-WHOO, TO-WHOO."
Up jumped the brownies and away they all flew (Make brownies back away from perch leaving only the owl sitting on his perch)

Pumpkin Time

October time is pumpkin time (Clasp hands before stomach like pumpkin)
The nicest time of year
When all the pumpkins light their eyes (Point to eyes)
And grin from ear to ear. (Point to each ear)
Because they know at Halloween
They'll have lots of fun
Peeking through the window panes (Peek about)
And watching people run. (Make fingers run)

Halloween Surprise

(Tune: Sing a Song of Sixpense)

First you take a pumpkin (Arms for large pumpkin before stomach)
Big and round and fat
Then you cut the top off (Pretend to slice)
That will make the hat (Hand on head)
Then you hollow out the
Nose and mouth and eyes. (Point to nose, mouth and eyes)
Show it to the children for (Resume first position)
Halloween surprise!

Cut Into a Pumpkin

Cut into a pumpkin, (Make motion as if cutting with forefinger)
Scoop it with a spoon. (Make scooping motion)
Carve a little mouth that turns
Endwise like a moon, (Form a half circle with thumb and forefinger)
Cut two eyes to twinkle (Make two circles with thumbs and forefingers)
And a big three-cornered nose. (Put forefingers and thumbs together to form a triangle)
Use for teeth ten shiny seeds
Placed in grinning rows. (Hold up ten fingers in a row)
Light a little candle;
And when the shadows fall (Hold up forefinger of left hand for a candle. Pretend to light it)
Set the jolly fellow
In the darkest hall. (Pretend to set pumpkin on shelf)
Listen for the laughter
As folks spy the elf, (Put one hand behind ear)
Grinning down at all of us
From the darkest shelf. (Put hands around face and smile)

This Little Pumpkin

This little pumpkin was taken to market (Pointer)
And sold for fifteen cents.
This little pumpkin was made into a jack-o-lantern (Middle finger)
And stood high on a fence.
This little pumpkin was made into a pie (Ring finger)
And nevermore was seen.
This little pumpkin was taken away (Little finger)
On the night of Halloween.

Pumpkin Parade

Five timid pumpkins
are marching in a row.
They have left the cornfield
Where they used to grow. (Fingers of right hand extended)
And now they're on the highway,
falling into line.
They must face the traffic
and not cry or whine. (Fingers "march" forward)
Suddenly a pumpkin
stumbles in a rut, (Bend the thumb)
Then another goes down;
his toe is cut. (Bend the index finger)
"This must be contagious,
says Jack as he falls. (Bend the middle finger)
"Two of us are left"
cries another and sprawls. (Bend the fourth finger)
But the last little pumpkin
continues, neat and clean,
And marches forward bravely
to arrive for Halloween. (Little finger continues to march)

I am Jolly Jack-O-Lantern

Ho! Ho! Little folks (Stand or sit with hands on hips)
Do not be afraid.
I am jolly jack-o-lantern
Out of a pumpkin made.
When I was a pumpkin fat, (Clasp hands before stomach in large pumpkin formation)
Out in the fields I lay, (Swing pumpkin out to left)
Until a little laddie came
And carried me away. (Move pumpkin slowly to right)
He cut a slit for each eye (Point to eyes)
And another for a nose (Point to nose)
Then carved a great big grinning mouth (Hold right forefinger before mouth)
With teeth in funny rows.
He put a candle in my head (Place candle on top of head)
And let the light stream through,
And said, "Oh, Jack-o-lantern, (Hands on hips)
Won't I have fun with you!"

What Makes You Run?

"What makes you run, my little man,
You are all out of breath?"
A pumpkin made a face at me
And scared me almost to death.

We Have a Pumpkin

We have a pumpkin, a big orange pumpkin,
We gave him two eyes to see where he goes.
We have him a mouth. We gave him a nose.
We put a candle in. Oh, see how he glows.

I Am a Pumpkin

I am a pumpkin big and round.
Once upon a time I grew on the ground.
But now I have a mouth, two eyes, and nose.
What are they for do you suppose?
When I have a candle inside, shining bright,
I'll be a jack-o-lantern on Halloween night.

Ten Little Pumpkins

Ten little pumpkins all in a line (Both hands up, fingers separated)
One ran away and then there were nine. (Curl fingers under as poem suggests)
Nine little pumpkins, who never were late
Off goes another! Now there are eight.
Eight little pumpkins, there never were eleven
Quietly another goes. Now there are seven.
Seven little pumpkins, full of 'jolly tricks
One jumps out of sight, then there are six.
Six little pumpkins, glad to be alive
One rolls away and then there are five.
Five little pumpkins, looking out the door.
Look! There goes another. Now there are four.
Four little pumpkins, as you can see.
But one slowly disappears, so now there are only three.
Three little pumpkins, feeling somewhat blue.
See, there goes another one, leaving only two.
Two little pumpkins alone in the sun.
Another says, "Goodby, friend" that leaves only one.
One little pumpkin, what shall he do?
The others all have run away and he will too.
Ten little pumpkins, "Oh, we had such fun (Both hands up again)
We'll skip and dance and play awhile (Flutter fingers)
Then run out in the sun." (Fingers run off)

Five Little Jack-O-Lanterns

Five little Jack-o-lanterns (One hand up)
Sitting on a gate.
The first one said (Point to thumb)
"My, it's getting late."
The second one said, (Pointer finger)
"I hear a noise."
The third one said, (Middle finger)
"It's just a lot of boys."
The fourth one said, (Ring finger)
"Come one, let's run"
The fifth one said (Little finger)
"It's just Halloween fun."
"Puff" went the wind
And out went the light (Close fingers into fist)
And away went the Jack-o-lanterns (Open hand, fingers run behind back)
Halloween night.

Once There Was a Pumpkin

Once there was a pumpkin
And it grew (Join the fingers of each hand to make one pumpkin)
And grew (Separate the hand keeping pumpkin formation)
And grew (Join hands before you, making large pumpkin with arms)
Now it's a jack-o-lantern
And smiles at you (Swing pumpkin to left)
And you (Move pumpkin before stomach)
And you (Swing pumpkin to the right)

Witch, Witch

Witch, witch, where do you fly?
Over the moon and under the sky.
Witch, witch what do you eat?
Little black apples from hurricane street.
Witch, witch, what do you drink?
Vinegar, blacking and good red ink.
Witch, witch, where do you sleep.
Up in the clouds where pillows are cheap.

Little Witches

One little, two little, three little witches (Hold up fingers one by one)
Ride through the sky on a broom; (Hands clasped together in front)
One little, two little, three little witches (Repeat action in line one)
Wink their eyes at the moon. (Wink one eye while making circle with arms)

Three Little Witches

One little, two little, three little witches,
Fly over haystacks, fly over ditches,
Slide down the moon without any hitches,
Hi, Ho, Halloween is here.

On Halloween

On Halloween, just take a peek
Wee brownies creep when we are asleep.
Elves and pixies dance and leap.
Witches ride upon a broom.
And fuzzy bats dart past me --- zoom!

Sitting on the Fence

What's that sitting on the fence up there?
My it gave me an awful scare!
"Meow, meow," Now what is that?
Just jolly jack-o-lantern and a big black cat.

A Funny Face

I've made a funny false face
With nose and mouth and eyes (Point to nose, mouth and eyes)
And when you see me wear it
You'll have a great surprise (Bring palms of hand together slowly in gesture of surprise)

For I shall put it on me (Lay hand on either cheek)
And look right straight at you
And in my loudest voice, I'll say (Open eyes wide)
"Boo! hoo! hoo! hoo! hoo! hoo!

Thanksgiving

Table Stretches

Every day when we eat our dinner,
Our table is very small. (Show size with hands)
There's room for daddy, (Hold up tall finger)
And mother, (Hold up pointer finger)
And baby, that is all, (Hold up little finger)
But when Thanksgiving Day comes
You can't believe your eyes.
For that table stretches (Stretch arms)
Until it is this size!

Five Little Pilgrims

Five little pilgrims on Thanksgiving Day; (Hold up one hand)
The first one said, "I'll have cake if I may." (Point to thumb)
The second one said, "I'll have turkey roasted." (Point to pointer finger)
The third one said, "I'll have chestnuts toasted." (Point to middle finger)
The fourth one said, "I'll have pumpkin pie." (Point to ring finger)
The fifth one said, "Oh cranberries I spy." (Point to little finger)
But before they ate the turkey or dressing,
All of the pilgrims said a Thanksgiving blessing. (Hands in prayer formation)

Wake Up, Little Pilgrim

Wake up, little pilgrims,
The sun's in the east. (Children sit tall)
Today is the day for our Thanksgiving feast. (Fold hands)
Come, jump out of bed,
See how tall you can stand. (Hold up ten fingers)
My, my, but you are a wide awake band!
Wash your hands, wash your faces, (Motion of washing)
So that you will look neat. (Fold hands in lap)
Then come to the table; say prayers before you eat. (Fold hands in prayer)

Mr. Duck

Mr. Duck went out to walk (Pointer finger)
In (snowy, blowy, bright sunshiny, very rainy, dark and cloudy) weather.
He met Mr. Turkey on the way. (Add middle finger)
They stopped and talked together.
Gobble! Gobble! Gobble! Quack! Quack! Quack! (Turkey and duck bob up and
Gobble! Gobble! Gobble! Quack! Quack! Quack! down)
And then they both went back. (Both fingers walk away)

Five Fat Turkeys

Five fat turkeys were sitting on a fence. (One hand up)
The first one said, "I'm so immense." (Point to thumb)
The second one said, "I can gobble at you." (Pointer finger)
The third one said, "I can gobble, too." (Middle finger)
The fourth one said, "I can spread my tail." (Ring finger)
The fifth one said, "Don't catch it on a nail." (Little finger)
A farmer came along and stopped to say (Pointer finger of other hand)
"Turkeys look best on Thanksgiving Day."

Variation of last two lines:
Out came the cook with a great big pan (Arms in pan form)
Away flew the turkeys, their tails in a fan. (Fingers fly away)

Five Little Turkeys

Five little turkeys flew up in a tree (One hand up)
The first one said, "There's a man I see." (Point to thumb)
The second one said, "He's coming this way." (Pointer finger)
The third one said, "It's Thanksgiving day." (Middle finger)
The fourth one said, "What's he going to do?" (Ring finger)
The fifth one said, "He's coming after you." (Little finger)
Chop went the axe before they flew away. (Clap hands on chop)
They all were on the table on Thanksgiving Day. (Make table of one hand for "turkeys" of other hand to sit)

Five Turkeys in a Tree

Five fat turkeys are we (One hand up)
We slept all night in a tree (Hands clasped above head)
When the cook came around
We couldn't be found,
That's why we're here, you see. (Right hand up)

To Grandma's House

Tune: The Farmer in the Dell

To Grandma's house we go (Make two fists and move them up and down as riding)
Heigh ho, heigh ho, heigh, ho.
We're on our way with horse and sleigh
Through fluffy drifts of snow.
Oh, what a trip to take!
She'll have a chocolate cake
There'll be some pies (Hands clasped before stomach)
Of monstrous size
And chestnuts we can bake.
To Grandma's house we go,
Heigh ho, heigh ho, heigh ho.
What lovely things Thanksgiving brings
The nicest things we know.

Thank-you

Mother, father, sister, brother, (Point to fingers one at a time)
Baby, too, will pray: (Place hands together in prayer)
"Thank thee, Heavenly Father,
On this fine Thanksgiving Day."

Christmas

Five Little Bells

Five little bells hanging in a row (Hold up hand)
The first one said, "Ring me slow." (Point to thumb)
The second one said, "Ring me fast." (Pointer)
The third one said, "Ring me last." (Middle finger)
The fourth one said, "I'm like a chime." (Ring finger)
The fifth one said, "Ring me at Christmas time." (Little finger)

Christmas Tree

Here is Bobby's Christmas tree (Stand right hand upright)
Standing right up tall.
Here's a pot to hold its trunk (Cup left hand under right hand)
So that it won't fall.
Here are balls to make it gay (Thumb and pointer fingers in ball formation)
One ball, two balls, see?
And here are two bright candles red (Right pointer and middle fingers upright)
To trim the Christmas tree.

Five Green Christmas Trees

Five green Christmas trees, fir and spruce and pine, (Five fingers up)
Waiting in the mountains till Christmas time.
The first one said, "I would like to live (Point to thumb)
With folks who have no present to give."
The second one said, "There's a tiny boy (Pointer finger)
In a hospital, I'll bring him joy."
The third one said, "There's a grandmother gray (Middle finger)
Who would like me to brighten her Christmas day."
The fourth one said, "On Christmas morn,
I'll remind everyone that Christ was born." (Ring finger)
The fifth and last raised his branches high (Little finger)
In a prayer of peace toward the Christmas sky.

Five Little Reindeer

One, two, three, four, five little reindeer (Hold up fingers, one at a time)
Stand beside the gate.
"Hurry Santa", said the five
"So we will not be late."
One, two, three, four, five little reindeer (Hold up fingers again)
Santa said, "Please wait,
Wait for three more reindeer, (Hold up three more fingers)
And then that will make eight.

Eight Tiny Reindeer

Eight tiny reindeer pawing in the snow,
Eight tiny reindeer ready to go;
This one has a shiny red nose;
He tells Santa which way the sleigh goes.
This one stamps the ice with his hoof;
He wants to hurry to Bobby's roof.
This one holds up his antlers high;
At a signal, he will be ready to fly!
This one looks all around to see
If there is a dolly for Sarah Lee.
This one stands at attention still
While Santa the sleigh with toys does fill.
This one pulls at the bit, for he
Wants to start on the long journey.
This one praces and jingles his bells
Santa, it's time to go he tells.
This one, last of the reindeer band,
Feels the reins pull in Santa's hands.
With a Hi, Hi, Ho! They are on their way,
And eight tiny reindeer pull the sleigh
To make children happy on Christmas day.

Here's Santa

Here's Santa, jolly and gay. (Hold up thumb on left hand)
He'll soon be on his way,
Here's Mrs. Santa, making toys (Hold up thumb on right hand)
For all good girls and boys,
Come Dancer, Prancer, Dasher, and Vixon, (Hold up four fingers on left hand: point to them)
Come Comet, Cupid, Donner and Blitzen, (Hold up four fingers on right hand: point to them)
Now, away to your housetop, (Point to a friend)
Clickety-clop, clickety-clop, clickety-clop. (Clapping motion, loud, soft, softer)

Santa's Workshop

In Santa's workshop far away.
Ten little elves work night and day. (Hold up ten fingers)
This little elf makes candy canes; (Point to little finger on one hand)
This little elf builds streamlined trains; (Point to ring finger)
This little elf paints dolls for girls; (Point to middle finger)
This little elf puts in their curls; (Point to pointer finger)
This little elf dips chocolate drops; (Point to thumb)
This little elf makes lollipops; (Point to little finger on other hand)
This little elf packs each jack-in-the-box; (Point to ring finger)
This little elf sews dolly socks; (Point to middle finger)
This little elf wraps books for boys; (Point to pointer finger)
This little elf checks off the toys; (Point to thumb)
As Santa packs them in his sleigh;
Ready for you on Christmas Day.

A Ride From Santa

If I could find old Santa, I'd ask him for a ride.
And in the wooly blankets, I'd snuggle by his side.
And when we go up high, to the chimneys tall,
I would stay up on the roof, for fear that I would fall.
And when the reindeer start to go.
I'd call out loudly, Whoa! Reindeer! Whoa!

Santa

When Santa comes down the chimney (Downward motion with hands)
I should like to peek (Peek through fingers)
But he'll never come, no never (Shake head)
Until I'm fast asleep. (Palms together beside head)

Here Is a Chimney

Here is a chimney deep and wide. (Raise arms straight up)
Do you think Santa can get inside?
Here is the fireplace warm and black (Forearms horizontal, middle fingers touching)
And here is old Santa's bursting pack. (Hand clasped before stomach)
Here are the stockings one – two – three; (Hold fingers up at each count)
Hanging side by side you see.
Here is the book that Santa bought (Hands side by side, palms up)
And here is the kite that Bobby bought. (Arms up fingertips touching)
Here is a ball so soft and round (Fingers touching in ball shape)
And here is a hammer pound, pound, pound. (One fist pounds other)
Here is a music box – clap, clap, clap, (Clap three times)
And here is a whip, just hear it snap. (Hold arm out and click fingernails)
A bag of candy for each girl and boy (Hold fists out)
Surely their hearts will fill with joy.
Then over the roof and far away,
Dashes old Santa and his sleigh. (Right pointer upright between left pointer and middle finger dash away)

Toy Shop

Here is a window in a Christmas toy shop (Make window with arms)
This is a round balloon that pops. (Make circle with hands, then clap)
This is a top that spins in a ring. (Indicate spinning motion with pointer fingers)
This is a little bird that can sing. (Whistle)
This is a little soldier who can walk. (March)
This is a momma doll that can talk. (Say "Momma")
This is a funny jumping jack man. (Squat and then jump up)
This is a sleepy Raggedy Ann. (Reach head and arms)
And now we will say good-bye to the toys (Wave)
And tip-toe away without any noise. (Tip toe)

This Little Present

This little present goes to Mary (Thumb)
This little present goes to Ned (Pointer)
This little present goes to Harry (Middle finger)
And this little present goes to Ted. (Ring finger)
This little present cried "Boo Hoo Hoo. (Little finger)
Please put me into the Christmas Stocking too!"

Clap Your Hands

Oh clap, clap your hands, and sing out, with glee, (Clap)
For Christmas is coming, and merry are we.
Now over the snow come Santa's reindeer
They scamper and scamper to bring Santa here.
We'll hang up our stockings and when we're asleep!
Down into our houses Old Santa will creep.
He'll fill all our stockings with presents and then
Santa Claus and his reindeer will scamper again,
So clap, clap your hands and sing out with glee (Clap)
For Christmas is coming and merry are we.

Valentine's Day

Five Little Valentines

Five little valentines were having a race
The first little valentine was frilly with lace. (Thumb)
The second little valentine had a funny face. (Pointer)
The third little valentine said, "I love you". (Middle finger)
The fourth little valentine said, "I do too". (Ring finger)
The fifth little valentine was sly as a fox; (Little finger)
He ran the fastest to your valentine box!

Pretty Valentine

To every little friend of mine,
I'll send a pretty valentine. (Make heart shape with thumbs and pointers)
You'll find a message, if you'll look. (Open palms)
I'll use an envelope for this. (Two fists together)
I'll write my name, then seal a kiss. (One hand closes on fingers of other hand)
What color shall I give to you?
Orange, purple, green, or blue?
Yellow or pink? White or red?
Or maybe a lacy one instead.

How Many Valentines?

Valentines, valentines;
How many do you see?
Valentines, valentines;
Count them with me:
    One for Father, (Hold up thumb)
    One for Mother, (Pointer finger)
    One for Grandma, too (Hold up middle finger)
    One for Sister, (Ring finger)
    One for Brother, (Little finger)
And here is one for you! (Make heart shape with thumbs and pointer fingers)

Gay Valentines

Five gay valentines (Hold up five fingers)
From the ten cent store
I sent one to Mother, (Bend down a finger)
Now there are four.
Four gay valentines
Pretty ones to see;
I give one to Brother, (Bend down finger)
Now there are three.
Three gay valentines,
Yellow, red and blue;
I give one to Sister (Bend down finger)
Now there are two.
Two gay valentines,
My, we have fun;
I give one to Daddy, (Bend down finger)
Now there is one.
One gay valentine,
The story is almost done;
I give it to Baby, (Bend down finger)
Now there are none.

Easter

Easter Eggs

Five little Easter eggs lovely colors wore; (Hold up five fingers)
Mother ate the blue one, then there were four (Bend down one finger)
Four little Easter eggs, two and two you see;
Daddy ate the red one, then there were three (Bend down one finger)
Three little Easter eggs; before I knew,
Sister ate the yellow one, then there were two. (Bend down one finger)
Two little Easter eggs, oh, what fun!
Brother ate the purple one, then there was one. (Bend down one finger)
One little Easter egg, see me run!
I ate the very last one, and then there were none. (Bend down last finger)

Go to Church

On Easter Day, we go to church. (Place two fists together)
The bell rings from the steeple. (Extend two pointer fingers to make steeple)
When the doors are opened wide, (Interlock fingers and turn hands so that fingers stand up)
Inside you'll see all the people.

Family of Rabbits

A family of rabbits lived under a tree; (Close right hand and hide it under left arm)
A father, a mother and babies three. (Hold up thumb, then fingers in succession)
Sometimes the bunnies would sleep all day; (Make fist)
But when night came, they liked to play. (Wiggle fingers)
Out of the hole they'd go creep, creep, creep. (Move fingers in creeping motion)
While the birds in the trees were all asleep. (Rest face on hands, place palms together)
Then the bunnies would scamper about and run, (Wiggle fingers)
Uphill, downhill! Oh, what fun! (Move fingers vigorously)
But when the mother said, "It's time to rest", (Hold up middle finger)
Pop! They would hurry (Clap hands after "pop")
Right back to their nest! (Hide hand under arm)

Five Little Rabbits

Five little rabbits under a log! (Hold up one hand)
This one said, "Shhh, I hear a dog!" (Point to thumb)
This one said, "I see a man!" (Pointer)
This one said, "Run while you can!" (Middle finger)
This one said, "I'm not afraid!" (Ring finger)
This one said, "Let's hide in the shade!" (Little finger)
A man and his dog went hurrying by,
And you should have seen those rabbits fly! (Place hand behind back quickly)

Chocolate Bunny

The sweet chocolate bunny poked out his head (Wrap fingers of left hand around right thumb; have end of thumb peeking out)
Then wiggled his ears (Wiggle second and third fingers of right hand)
"It's Easter", he said.
"And good boys and girls are waiting to see
What sweet chocolate bunny (Cup fingers of left hand and pretend to put something in it with right hand)
Will hide in his tree."
The hen said, "Basket of eggs (Interlock fingers of hands to make a basket)
I'll give you."
The honey bee said, "I've paste (Cup fingers of right hand)
for you, too."
The warm shining sun said, (Form a circle with the fingers of both hands)
"And for my good deed
I'll melt all the chocolate
that you're going to need."
So the sweet chocolate bunny (Join right index finger and thumb in gesture of holding a brush)
With his tail for a brush
Painted each egg
With sweet chocolate mush
And then with his whiskers
And honey bee paste
The name of a child (Pretend to write on back of left fist with right hand)
On each egg he traced.

Easter Rabbit

A rabbit came to my house once,
With funny, stretched–out ears. (Hands on head like bunny ears)
His nose was full of wriggles, and (Wiggle nose)
His eyes were full of fears (Point to eyes)
I said, "Why do you twitch your nose?
Is that a bunny habit?
And are you called the 'March Hare'
Or called the 'Easter Rabbit'?"
He never said a word; but bounced (Hands on head like bunny ears)
Away on pushing legs; (Hop forward)
But, oh, he left behind a nest (Look backward over a shoulder)
Of colored Easter eggs!

Bunny In The Wood

There was a bunny who lived in the wood.
He wiggled his ears as a good bunny should (Forefinger on either side of head for ears)
He hopped by a squirrel (Hold two fingers up and close others on one hand and take one jump down other arm)
He hopped by a tree (Take another hop)
He hopped by a duck (Take another hop)
And he hopped by me. (Hop over the opposite fist)
He stared at the squirrel,
He stared at the tree,
He stared at the duck,
But he made faces at me. (Wiggle nose)

Sweet Bunny

There is nothing so sweet as a bunny (Hands on head for bunny ears)
A dear, little, sweet, little bunny.
He can hop on his toes (Hop forward)
He can wiggle his nose (Wiggle nose)
And his powder puff tail is quite funny. (Ball formation with hands)

Make a Rabbit

Oh, can you make a rabbit (Pointer and middle fingers up)
With two ears, so very long?
And let him hop, hop, hop about (Rabbit hoos)
On legs so small and strong?
He nibbles, nibbles carrots (Insert second finger of left hand for the carrot between the thumb, forth and fifth fingers of the right hand representing the mouth. Open and close the fingers to imitate nibbling)
For his dinner every day.
As soon as he has had enough
He scampers far away. (Rabbit scampers away)

Hop!

Creeping, creeping, creeping (Walk two fingers down other arm)
Comes a little cat.
But bunny with his long ears (Pointer and middle finger up for ears)
Hops! Like that! (Pointer and middle finger hop down other arm)

Ears So Funny

Here is a bunny with ears so funny (Right fist with two fingers raised)
And here is his home in the ground (Cup left hand)
When a noise he hears, he pricks up his ears,
And he jumps to his home in the ground. (Right two fingers dive into cupped left hand)

Cabbage Head

Once there was a rabbit (Pointer and middle fingers up)
And a green cabbage head (Fish of left hand)
"I think I'll have some breakfast."
So he nibbled and he nibbled (Rabbit nibble cabbage)
And he cocked his head to say,
"I guess this little rabbit
Should hop–hop–hop away." (Rabbit hops away)

Robbie the Rabbit

Robbie the Rabbit is fat, fat, fat (Pat stomach)
His soft little paws go pat, pat, pat (Pat hands)
His soft little ears go flop, flop, flop (Hands on head – flop hands)
And when Robbie runs, he goes hop, hop, hop. (Hop forward three times)

Bunnies

"Come my bunnies, it's time for bed,"
That's what mother bunny said,
"But first I'll count you just to see
If you have all come back to me;
Bunny one, Bunny two, Bunny three, Bunnies so dear,
Bunny four, Bunny five, Yes, You're all here.
You're all here.
You're the sweetest things alive
My bunnies, one, two, three, four, five."

Twelve Little Rabbits

Twelve little rabbits in a rabbit pen;
Two hopped away and then there were ten (Hold up ten fingers)
Ten little rabbits with ears up straight;
Two hopped away and then there were eight. (Bend down two fingers)
Eight little rabbits doing funny tricks;
Two hopped away and then there were six. (Bend down two fingers)
Six little rabbits eating carrots from the store;
Two hopped away and then there were four. (Bend down two fingers)
Four little rabbits looked for gardens new;
Two hopped away and then there were two. (Bend down two fingers)
Two little rabbits found a new friend;
They hopped away, and that is the end. (Bend down last two fingers)

This Little Bunny

This little bunny has two pink eyes; (Pointer)
This little bunny is very wise; (Middle finger)
This little bunny is soft as silk; (Ring finger)
This little bunny is white as milk; (Little finger)
This little bunny nibbles away (Thumb)
At cabbages and carrots the live long day!

Five Little Easter Rabbits

Five little Easter rabbits (Hold up five fingers)
Sitting by the door;
One hopped away, and then there were four. (Bend down one finger)

Refrain:

Hop, hop, hop, hop; (Clap on each hop)
See how they run!
Hop, hop, hop, hop! (Clap on each hop)
They think it's great fun!

Four little Easter rabbits (Hold up four fingers)
Under a tree;
One hopped away, and then there were three. (Bend down one finger)

Repeat refrain

Three little Easter rabbits (Hold up three fingers)
Looking at you;
One hopped away, and then there were two. (Bend down one finger)

Repeat refrain

Five Little Easter Rabbits – Continued

Two little Easter rabbits (Hold up two fingers)
Resting in the sun;
One hopped away, and then there was one. (Bend down one finger)

Repeat refrain

One little Easter rabbit
Left all alone;
He hopped away, and then there were none. (Hand behind back)

Last refrain

Hop, hop, hop, hop! (Clap on each hop)
All gone away!
Hop, hop, hop, hop! (Clap on each hop)
They'll come back some day.

Birthdays

My Birthday Cake

My birthday cake is pink and white; (Make a circle with arms)
The lighted candles make it bright;
One, two, three, four, five pink candles! (Hold up fingers one by one to represent candles)
What a pretty sight!

Polly's Birthday

Polly had a birthday;
Polly had a cake; (Make a circle with arms)
Polly's mother made it; (Action of stirring)
Polly watched it bake.
Frosting on the top, (Right hand held out, palm down)
Frosting in between; (Left hand moves under right palm)
Oh, it was the nicest cake
That you have ever seen!
Polly had some candles,
One, two, three, four, five; (Hold up fingers one at a time)
Who can tell how many years
Polly's been alive?

Look at Me

Please everybody look at me (Point to self)
Today I'm five year's old you see (Hold one hand up)
And after this I won't be four (Hold four fingers up)
Not ever, ever any more?

I won't be three (Three fingers up)
or two (Two fingers)
or one. (One finger)
For that was when I'd first begun.
Now I'll be five for awhile, and then (Five fingers up again)
I'll be something else again.

Today's Birthday

Today is ___________________'s birthday; (Insert the name of the child)
Let's make her (him) a cake;
Mix and stir, (Action of stirring)
Stir and mix,
Then into the oven to bake. (Pretend to hold the cake in two hands)
Here's our cake so nice and round: (Make a circle with arms)
We frost it pink and white; (Action of spreading frosting)
We put six (any number) candles on it,
To make a birthday light.

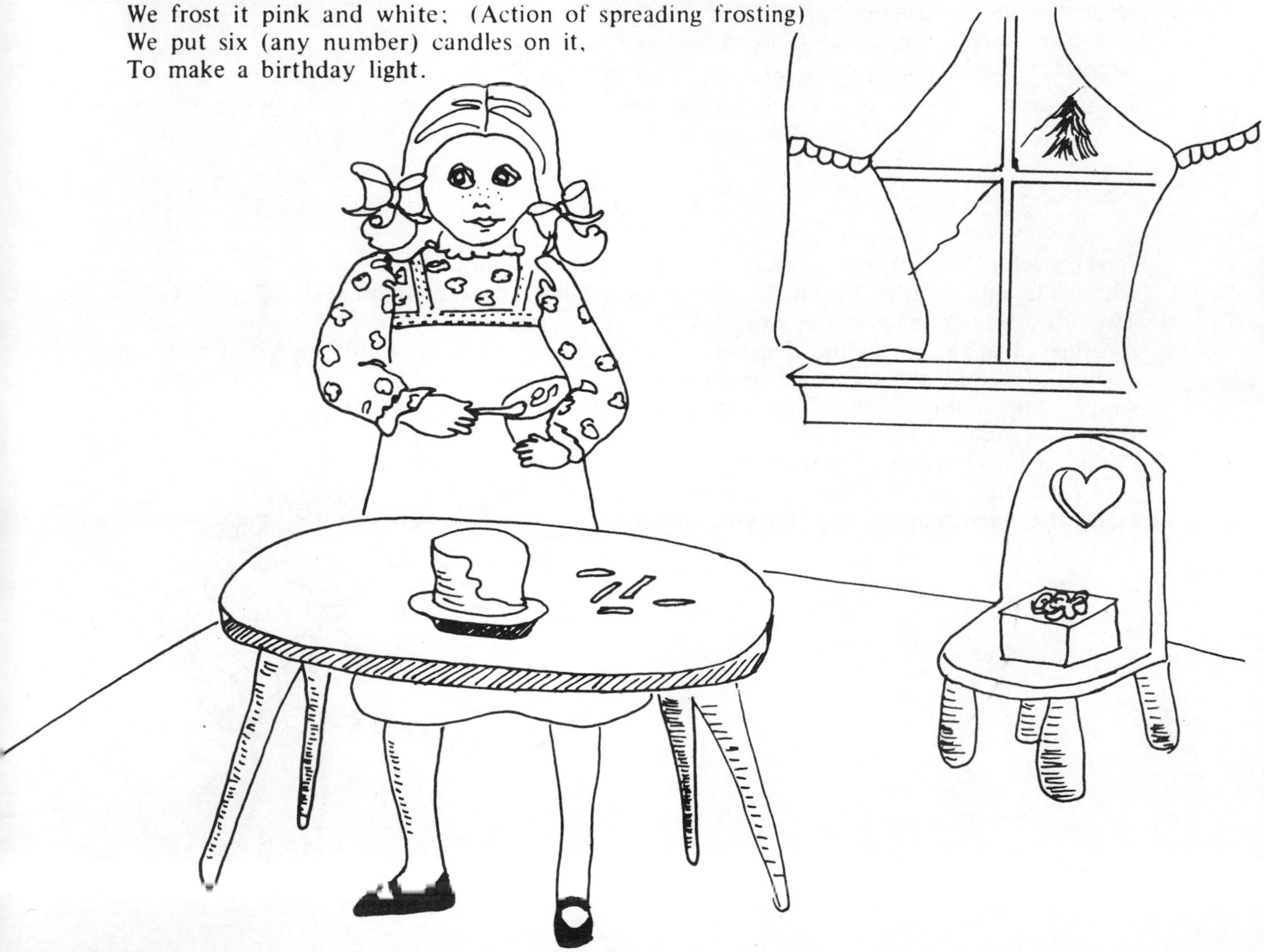

THE WORLD AROUND US

Animals

Five Busy Bees

Five little busy bees on a day so sunny; (Hold up all fingers on one hand)
Number one said, "I'd like to make some honey." (Bend down first finger)
Number two said, "Tell me, where shall it be?" (Bend down second finger)
Number three said, "In the old honey-tree." (Bend down third finger)
Number four said, "Let's gather pollen sweet." (Bend down fourth finger)
Number five said, "Let's take it on our feet." (Bend down thumb)
Humming their busy little honey-bee song,
"Bzzzzzzzzzzzzzzzzzzzzzzzzz!"

Bees

There is a beehive (Hand cupped)
Where are the bees?
Hidden away where nobody sees.
Now they come creeping out of the hive
One, two, three, four, five. (Extend fingers one by one)
Bzzzzzzzzzzzzzzzzzzzzzzzzz!

Little Bird

One little bird with lovely feathers blue (Hold up first finger)
Sat beside another one. Then there were two. (Hold up second finger)
Two little birds singing in the tree.
Another came to join them. Then there were three. (Hold up third finger)
Three little birds, wishing there were more;
Along came another bird. Then there were four. (Hold up fourth finger)
Four little birds, glad to be alive
Found a lonely friend. Then there were five. (Hold up thumb)
Five little birds just as happy as can be
Five little birds singing songs for you and me.

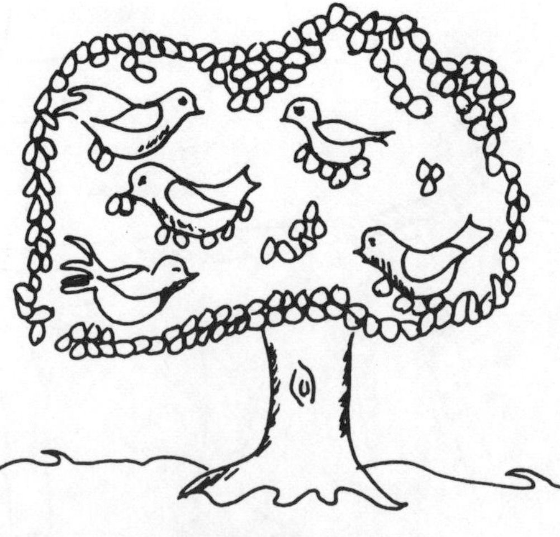

Chickadees

Five little chickadees sitting in a door; (Hold up hand)
One flew away and then there were four. (Put down one finger at a time)
Four little chickadees sitting in a tree;
One flew away and then there were three.
Three little chickadees looking at you;
One flew away and then there were two.
Two little chickadees sitting in the sun;
One flew away and then there was one.
One little chickadee sitting all alone;
He flew away and then there were none.

Mrs. Pigeon

Mrs. Peck Pigeon
Is pecking for bread
Bob–bob–bob (Bob head up and down)
Goes her little round head.
Tame as a pussy cat
In the street,
Step, step, step (Take three steps)
Go her little red feet.
With her little red feet (Point to feet)
And her little round head (Point to head)
Mrs. Peck Pigeon
Goes pecking for bread.

Robins

Five little robins in a sycamore tree.
A father (Hold up thumb)
A mother (Hold up pointer finger)
And babies three; (Hold up remaining three fingers)
Father brought a worm: (Point to thumb)
Mother brought a bug; (Point to pointer finger)
The three baby robins started to tug;
This one ate the bug (Point to middle finger)
This one ate the worm (Point to ring finger)
And this one sat and waited for his turn. (Point to little finger)

Caterpillars

"Let's go to sleep", the little caterpillars said, (Bend ten fingers into palms)
As they tucked themselves into their beds.
They will awaken by and by, (Slowly unfold and hold up fingers)
And each one will be a lovely butterfly! (Hands make flying motion)

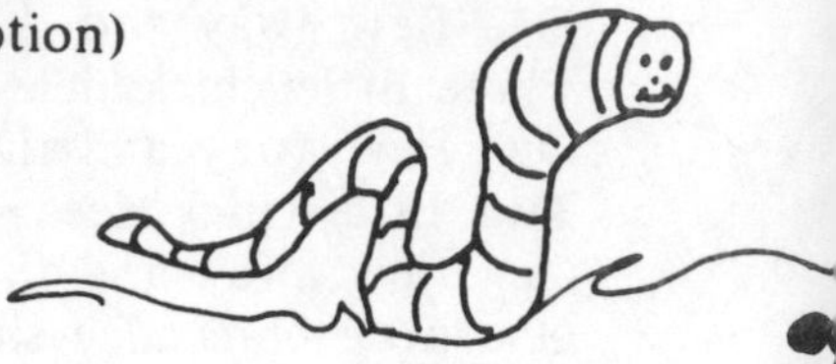

Pussy Cat

Softly, softly creeps the pussy cat. (Creep fingers on lap)
But the bunny with his two long ears (Hold two fingers in air)
Hops like that!

Little Cats

One little cat and two little cats
went for a romp one day.
One little cat and two little cats
make how many cats at play? (3)
Three little cats had lots of fun
till growing tired, away ran (1)
I really think he was most unkind to the
(2) little cats
That were left behind.

Pussy

This little pussy drinks her milk.
This little pussy's fur is like silk.
This little pussy wears soiled clothes
This little pussy is Scratch toes!
This little pussy can purr and sing
Oh, she can do most anything.

A Kitten

A kitten is fast asleep under the chair (Thumb under hands)
And Donald can't find her.
He's looked everywhere. (Fingers circling eyes to look)
Under the table, (Peek under one hand)
And under the bed. (Peek under other hand)
He looked in the corner and then Donald said,
"Come Kitty, come Kitty, this milk is for you." (Curve hands for dish)
And out came the kitty, calling "Meow, Meow." (Thumb walks across lap)

This Is a Pussy

This is a pussy, sleek and gray (Hold up one thumb)
With her kittens four. (Hold up four fingers)
She went to sleep on the floor (Close eyes)
By the kitchen door.

Little Chick

This little chick had corn today. (Point to fingers, one at a time)
This little chick had only hay.
This little chick had worms, they say.
This little chick cried, "Peep, peep, peep"
Feed me or I'll weep, weep, weep.
This little chick had feather shoes
He wore them out to get the news.

This Little Cow

This little cow eats grass; (Hold up one hand, fingers erect, bend down one finger)
This little cow eats hay; (Bend down another finger)
This little cow drinks water, (Bend down another finger)
And this little cow runs away (Bend down another finger)
This little cow does nothing (Bend down last finger)
But lie and sleep all day.

Froggies

This little froggie broke his toe (Point to one finger at a time)
This little froggie said, "Oh, oh, oh."
This little froggie laughed and was glad.
This little froggie cried and was sad.
This little froggie did just what he should,
Hopped straight to his mother as fast as he could. (Hop fingers away)

Ten Little Froggies

Ten little froggies were swimming in a pool; (Hold up ten fingers)
This little froggie said, "Let's go to school!" (Point to thumb)
This little froggie said, "Oh, yes! Let's go!" (Point to pointer finger)
This little froggie said, "We'll sit in a row." (Point to middle finger)
This little froggie siad, "We'll learn to read." (Point to ring finger)
This little froggie said, "Yes, yes indeed." (Point to little finger)
This little froggie said, "We'll learn to write." (Point to other thumb)
This little froggie said, "We'll try with all our might." (Point to pointer finger)
This little froggie said, "We will draw and sing." (Point to middle finger)
This little froggie said, "We'll learn EVERYTHING!" (Point to ring finger)
We'll come back here and swim in our pool. (Point to little finger)

Mice

Five little mice on the pantry floor; (Hold up five fingers)
This little mouse peeked behind the door; (Bend down little finger)
This little mouse nibbled at the cake; (Bend down ring finger)
This little mouse not a sound did make; (Bend down middle finger)
This little mouse took a bite of cheese; (Bend down pointer finger)
This little mouse heard the kitten sneeze. (Bend thumb down)
"Ah-Choo!" sneezed the kitten, and "Squeak!" they cried.
As they found a hole and ran inside. (Make running motions with fingers and hide hands behind back)

Baby Mice

Where are the baby mice?
Squeak, squeak, squeak! (Make fist and hide it behind you)
I cannot see them;
Peek, peek, peek! (Show fist and extend it)
Here they come out of their hole in the wall.
One, two, three, four, five, and that is all! (Show one finger at a time)

This Little Pig

This little pig went to market, (Point to one finger at a time)
This little pig stayed home,
This little pig had roast beef,
This little pig had none,
This little pig cried "Wee, wee, weee."
And ran all the way home.

Piggies

"It's time for my piggies to go to bed,"
The nice big mother piggie said.
"Now I must count them up to see
If all my piggies came back to me.
One little piggy, two little piggies,
Three little piggies dear;
Four little piggies, five little piggies –
Yes, they all are here.
They're the dearest little piggies alive –
One, two, three, four, five."

Pigs

Piggie Wig (Thumb) and Piggie Wee (Other thumb)
Hungry pigs as pigs could be
For their dinner had to wait
Down behind the garden gate (Gate made of fingers)
Piggie Wig and Piggie Wee (Wiggle thumbs as named)
Climbed the barnyard gate to see. (Thumbs through fingers)

Peeking through the gate so high
But no dinner could they spy,
Piggie Wig and Piggie Wee got down
Sad as pigs could be,
But the gate soon opened wide
And they scampered forth outside. (Hands swing apart, thumbs run)

Piggie Wig and Piggie Wee,
Greedy pigs as pigs could be
For their dinner ran pell mell
And in the trough both piggies fell. (Make trough with hands, thumbs fall in)

Eight Pigs

Two mother pigs lived in a pen, (Thumb)
Each had four babies and that made ten. (Fingers of both hands)
These four babies were black and white. (Fingers of one hand)
These four babies were black as night. (Fingers of the other hand)
All eight babies loved to play. (Wiggle fingers)
And they rolled and they rolled in the mud all day. (Roll hands)

Not Say a Single Word

We'll hop, hop, hop like a bunny (Make hopping motion with hand)
And run, run, run like a dog; (Make running motion with fingers)
We'll walk, walk, walk like an elephant, (Make walking motion with arms)
And jump, jump, jump like a frog, (Make jumping motions with arms)
We'll swim, swim, swim like a goldfish, (Make swimming motion with hand)
And fly, fly, fly like a bird; (Make flying motion with arms)
We'll sit right down and fold our hands, (Fold hands in lap)
And not say a single word!

Bunny

Here is a bunny with ears so funny (Right fist with two fingers raised)
And here is his home in the ground (Cup left hand)
When a noise he hears, he pricks up his ears,
And he jumps to his home in the ground (Right two fingers dive into cupped left hand)

A Bunny

Once there was a bunny (Fist with two fingers tall)
And a green, green cabbage head (Fish of other hand)
"I think I'll have some breakfast," This little bunny said.
So he nibbled, and he cocked his ears to say.
"I think it's time that I be on my way."

Five Little Squirrels

Five little squirrels sat up in a tree; (Hold up five fingers)
This little squirrel said, "What do I see?" (Point to thumb)
This little squirrel said, "I smell a gun!" (Point to pointer finger)
This little squirrel said, "Oh, let's run!" (Point to middle finger)
This little squirrel said, "Let's hide in the shade!" (Point to ring finger)
This little squirrel said, "I'm not afraid!" (Point to little finger)
Then BANG went the gun! (Clap hands)
And away the little squirrels ran, every one. (Make running motions with fingers)

Squirrel in a Tree

This is the squirrel that lives in a tree; (Make fist; hold two fingers erect)
This is the tree which he climbs; (Motion of fingers climbing up opposite arm)
This is the nut that he takes from me, (Make small circle)
As I sit very still sometimes. (Fold hands)

Little Toad

I am a little toad,
Hopping down the road. (Make fingers hop in time to verses)
Just listen to my song;
I sleep all winter long; (Palms together at side of head)
When spring comes, I peep out (Peep behind hands)
And then I jump about; (Make arms jump)
And now I catch a fly, (Clap hands)
And now I wink my eye (Wink one eye)
And now and then I hop (Make hands hop)
And now and then I stop. (Fold hands)

A Little Turtle

There was a little turtle,
He lived in a box. (Cup hands together for box)
He swam in a puddle, (Wiggle hand for swimming motion)
He climbed on the rocks. (Fingers climb up other fist)
He snapped at a mosquito, (Make snapping motion with thumb and fingers)
He snapped at a flea, (Snapping motion)
He snapped at a minnow, (Snapping motion)
And he snapped at me. (Snapping motion)
He caught the mosquito, (Clap)
He caught the flea, (Clap)
He caught the minnow, (Clap)
But he didn't catch me! (Move pointer finger back and forth)

Circus and Zoo

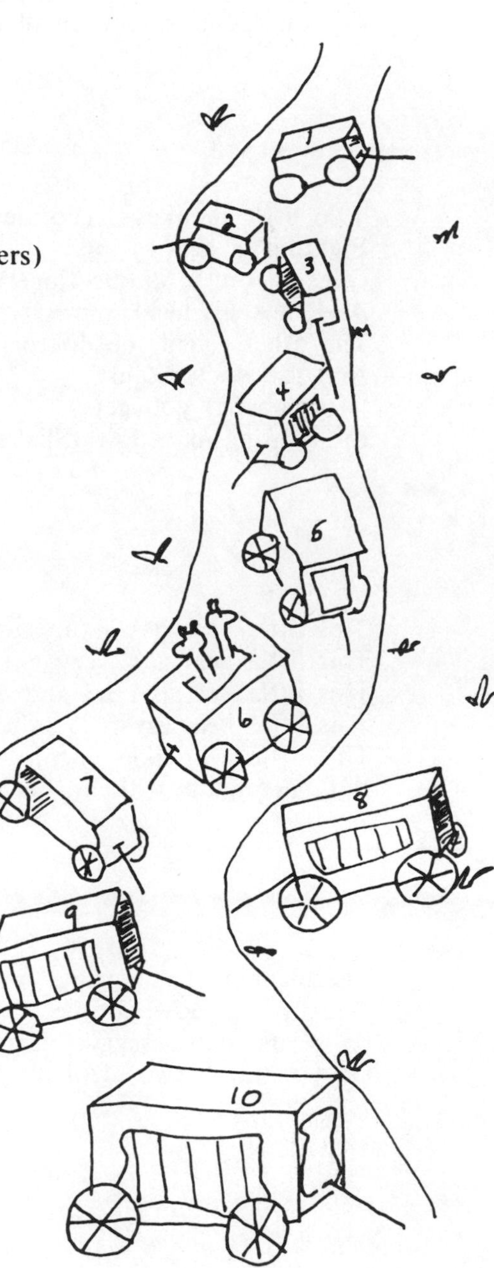

Ten Circus Wagons

Ten circus wagons, painted oh so gay,
Came into town with the circus today! (Hold up ten fingers)
This one holds a lion
That gives a big, loud roar! (Point to thumb)
This one holds a tiger
Fast asleep upon the floor. (Pointer finger)
This one holds a funny seal
That nods to left and right. (Middle finger)
This one holds a zebra
That is striped all black and white. (Ring finger)
This one holds a camel
With two humps upon his back. (Little finger)
This one holds a panther
With his coat of fur so black. (Thumb of other hand)
This one holds an elephant
That is drinking from a pail. (Pointer finger)
This one holds a monkey
That is swinging by his tail. (Middle finger)
This one holds a hippo
With a grin so very wide. (Ring finger)
This one holds a leopard
With a gaily spotted hide. (Little finger)
Ten circus wagons, painted oh so gay,
Came into town with the circus today! (Ten fingers)

This Little Clown

This little clown is fat and gay; (Thumb)
This little clown does tricks all day; (Pointer finger)
This little clown is tall and strong; (Middle finger)
This little clown is wee and small, (Ring finger)
But he can do anything at all! (Little finger)

Seals

The seals all flap their shining flips (Put hands under arms and flap arms)
And bounce balls on their nosey tips, (Point to nose)
And beat a drum and catch a bar, (Beat a drum)
And wriggle with how pleased they are. (Wriggle)

This Little Tiger

This little tiger is very wild, (Thumb)
This little tiger is a loving child. (Pointer finger)
This little tiger has some big black spots, (Middle finger)
This little tiger has small back dots; (Ring finger)
This little tiger likes to prowl and smell, (Little finger)
But his teeth are too small to bite very well.

Two Little Monkeys

Two little monkeys (Pointer and middle finger up)
Fighting in bed.
One fell out (Middle finger down)
And hurt his head
The other called the doctor (Pointer finger of other hand)
And the doctor said:
"That's what you get
for fighting in bed." (Shake "doctor" finger at "monkeys")

This Little Bear

This little bear has a fur suit, (Thumb)
This little bear acts very cute. (Pointer finger)
This little bear is bold and cross, (Middle finger)
This little bear says, "You're not boss." (Ring finger)
This little bear likes bacon and honey; (Little finger)
But he can't buy them, he has no money!

The Elephant

The elephant has a trunk for a nose, (Pretend an arm is the trunk)
And up and down is the way it goes; (Move arm up and down)
He wears such a saggy, baggy hide
Do you think two elephants would fit inside?

The Elephant's Trunk

The elephant has a great big trunk (Pretend an arm is the trunk)
That goes swinging, swinging so. (Swing trunk)
He has tiny, tiny eyes that show him where to go. (Point to eyes)
His huge long ears go flapping, flapping up and down, (Pretend hands are ears)
His great feet go stomping, stomping on the ground. (Stomp with feet)

Five Gray Elephants

Five gray elephants marching through a glade (March fingers of right hand)
Decide to stop and play they are having a parade.
The first swings his trunk and announces he'll lead, (Swing arm like trunk)
The next waves a flag which of course they need. (Wave hand over head)
The third gray elephant trumpets a song, (Blow through hand)
The fourth beats a drum as he marches along. (Beat a drum)
While the fifth makes believe he's the whole show
And nods and smiles to the crowd as they go. (Nod head to left and right and smile)
Five gray elephants marching through the glade
Having a lot of fun during their parade.

A Little Monkey

A little monkey likes to do
Just the same as you and you; (Point to two children)
When you sit up very tall, (Perform each action as indicated)
Monkey sits up very tall;
When you pretend to throw a ball,
Monkey pretends to throw a ball;
When you try to touch your toes,
Monkey tries to touch his toes;
When you move your little nose,
Monkey tries to move his nose;
When you jump up in the air,
Monkey jumps up in the air;
When you sit down in a chair;
Monkey sits down in a chair.

The Yellow Giraffe

The yellow giraffe is tall as can be, (Put hand up high)
His lunch is a bunch of leaves off a tree. (Put arm up for tree branches)
He has a very long neck and his legs are long too, (Point to neck and legs)
And he can run faster than his friends in the zoo. (Run in place)

The Funny Fat Walrus

The funny, fat walrus sits in the sea
Where the weather is freezing and cold as can be. (Put hands on arms and shiver)
His whiskers are droopy and his tusks are white
And he doesn't do much but sit day and night.

The Brown Kangaroo

The brown kangaroo is very funny
She leaps and runs and hops like a bunny. (Hop)
And on her stomach is a pocket so wide, (Put hand on stomach like a pocket)
Her baby can jump in and go for a ride. (Have other hand jump into "pocket")

The Kangaroo

Said the kind kangaroo,
"What can I do? (Hold out hands with palms up)
If I had a cradle, I'd rock it. (Cup hands and move back and forth)
But my baby is small
So I think after all,
I'll carry him 'round in my pocket!" (Put one hand on stomach for a pocket and put the other inside "pocket")
Jump, jump, jump goes the big kangaroo. (Jumping motion with pointer and middle fingers; other fingers and thumb folded)
I thought there was one, but I see there are two
The mother and a baby, See his head pop out, (Thumb comes between pointer and middle finger)
Of her cozy pocket, while he looks about
Yes, he can see what's going on
As his mother jumps along (Repeat jumping motion with thumb showing)
Jump, jump, jump,
Jump, jump, jump,
Jump, jump, jump.

Five Little Polar Bears

Five little polar bears, (Hold up one hand)
Playing on the shore;
One fell in the water
And then there were four. (Put down one finger as you say each verse)

Four little polar bears,
Swimming out to sea;
One got lost,
And then there were three.

Three little polar bears said
"What shall we do?"
One climbed an iceberg
Then there were two.

Two little polar bears
Playing in the sun;
One went for food,
Then there was one.

One little polar bear,
Didn't want to stay;
He said, "I'm lonesome,"
And swam far away.

The Zoo

This is the way the elephant goes, (Clasp hands together, extend arms, and move them back and forth)
With curly trunk instead of a nose.
The buffalo, all shaggy and fat,
Has two sharp horns in place of a hat. (Point fingers to forehead)
The hippo with his mouth so wide
Lets you see what is inside. (Hands together and open and close them to simulate mouth movements)
The wiggly snake upon the ground
Crawls along without a sound. (Weave hands back and forth)
But monkey see and monkey do
Is the funniest animal in the zoo. (Place thumbs in ears and wiggle hands)

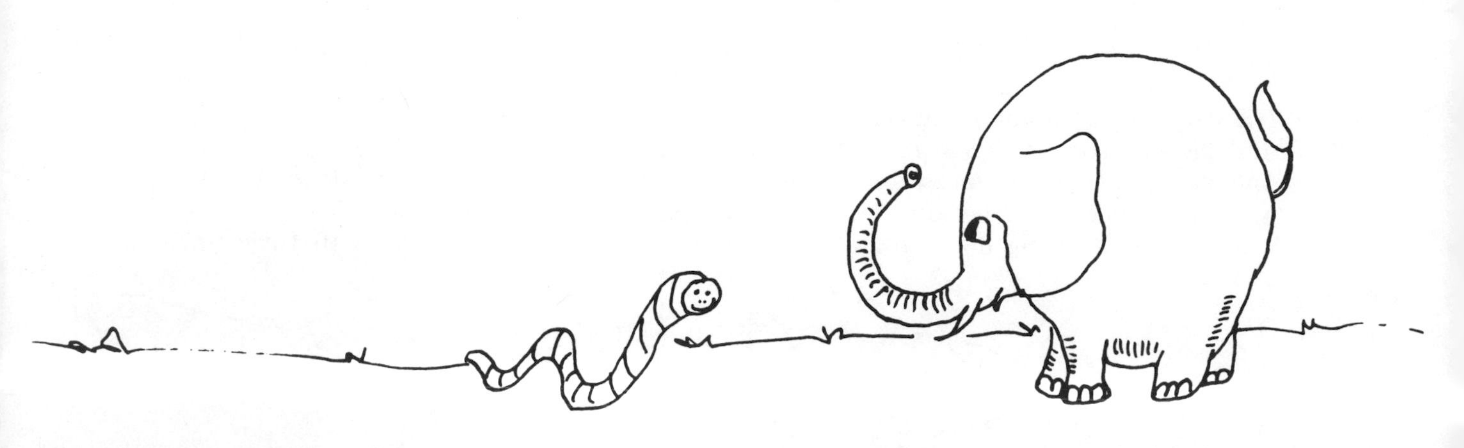

One, One; The Zoo is Lots of Fun

One, one; the zoo is lots of fun! (Hold up hands with fingers extended; bend down one finger as you say each line)
Two, two; see a kangaroo.
Three, three; see a chimpanzee.
Four, four; hear the lions roar.
Five, five; watch the seals dive.
Six, six; there's a monkey doing tricks.
Seven, seven; elephants eleven.
Eight, eight; a tiger and his mate.
Nine, nine; penguins in a line.
Ten, ten; I want to come again.

Community Helpers

Baker's Truck

The baker man's truck comes down the street
Filled with everything good to eat;
Two doors the baker man opens wide: (Stretch arms apart)
Now, let us look at the shelves inside.
What do you see? What do you see? (Hands over eyes)
Doughnuts and cookies for you and me: (Make circles with thumbs and pointers)
Cinnamon rolls, (Make larger circles)
And pies, (Make even larger circles)
And bread too;
What will he sell to me and to you?

The Carpenter

This is the way he saws the wood (Right hand saws left palm)
Sawing, sawing, sawing;
This is the way he nails a nail (Pound right fist on left palm)
Nailing, nailing, nailing;
This is the way he paints the house (Right hand paints left palm)
Painting, painting, painting.

Carpenter

The carpenter's hammer goes tap, tap, tap, (Pound fists together)
And his saw goes see, saw, see (Right hand saws left arm)
And he planes and he measures (Bend fingers of right hand and slide down left arm)
And he hammers and he saws (Hammer and saw as in above)
While he builds a big house for me. (Elbows bent, forearms upright with fingertips touching)

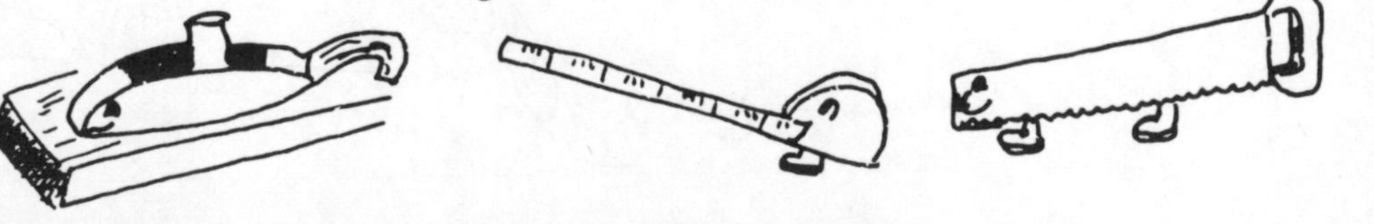

Ten Brave Firemen

Ten brave firemen sleeping in a row, (Fingers curled to make sleeping men)
Ding, dong, goes the bell, (Pull down on the bell cord)
And down the pole they go. (With fists together make hands slide down pole)
Off on the engine oh, oh, oh. (Pretend you are steering fire engine very fast)
Using the big hose, so, so, so. (Make a nozzle with fist to use hose)
When all the fire's out, home so-o-slow.
Back to bed, all in a row. (Curl all fingers again for sleeping men)

Five Little Firemen

Five little firemen sit very still (Hold up five fingers)
Until they see a fire on top of the hill;
Number one rings the bell, ding–dong; (Bend down thumb)
Number two pulls his big boots on (Bend down pointer finger)
Number three jumps on the fire engine red; (Bend down middle finger)
Number four puts a red fire hat on his head; (Bend down ring finger)
Number five drives the red fire truck to the fire, (Bend down little finger)
As the big yellow flames go higher and higher. (Spread arms)
Whoooooo-ooooo! Whoooooo-ooooo! Hear the fire truck say, (Imitate siren)
As all of the cars get out of the way.
Shhh! Goes the water from the fire hose spout, (Rub palms together)
And quicker than a wink the fire is out! (Clap hands)

Mail

Five little letters lying on a tray. (Extend fingers of right hand)
Mommy came in and took the first away. (Bend down thumb)
Then Daddy said, "This big one is for me."
I counted them twice now there were three. (Bend down pointer finger)
Brother Bill asked, "Did I get any mail?"
He found one and cried, "A letter from Gale!" (Bend down middle finger)
My sister Jane took the next to the last.
And ran upstairs to open it fast. (Bend down ring finger)
As I can't read, I'm not able to see
Whom the last one's for, but I hope it's for me! (Wiggle the little finger, then clap hands)

Traffic Policeman

The traffic policeman holds up his hand, (Hold up hand, palm forward)
He blows the whistle, (Pretend to blow whistle)
He gives the command. (Hold up hand again)
When the cars are stopped. (Hold up hand again)
He waves at me.
Then I may cross the street you see. (Wave hand as if indicating for someone to go)

Five Strong Policemen

Five strong policemen standing by a store. (Hold up fingers of one hand)
One became a traffic cop, and then there were four. (Bend down one finger)
Four strong policemen watching over me.
One took home a lost boy, and then there were three. (Bend one finger)
Three strong policemen dressed all in blue,
One stopped a speeding car, and then there were two. (Bend another finger)
Two strong policemen saw some smoke one day,
They called the firemen who put out the fire right away.

Safety

Light the Fire

Such jolly fun to rake the leaves (Make raking motion with arms)
And see the pile grow higher (Continue raking)
But always wait 'til Daddy comes (Shake right forefinger)
Before you light the fire. (Continue shaking forefinger)

Stood Up Dangerously

Silly little Teddy Bear
Stood up in a rocking chair. (Make rocking movement)
Now he has to stay in bed (Lay head on hands)
With a bandage 'round his head. (Circular movement of hand about head)

Look Both Ways

Step on the corner
Watch for the light.
Look to the left,
Look to the right.
If nothing is coming
Then start and don't talk
Go straight across
Be careful and walk.

Walking Home

When I walk home from school today,
I'll walk the safe and careful way.
I'll look to the left – I'll look to the right.
Then cross the street when no car is in sight.

Corner

Little Jack Horner stood on the corner (Stand with feet together)
Watching the traffic go by (Look to left and right)
And when it passed, he crossed at last (Take two steps forward)
And said, 'What a safe boy am I." (Thumbs under arms')

At the Curb

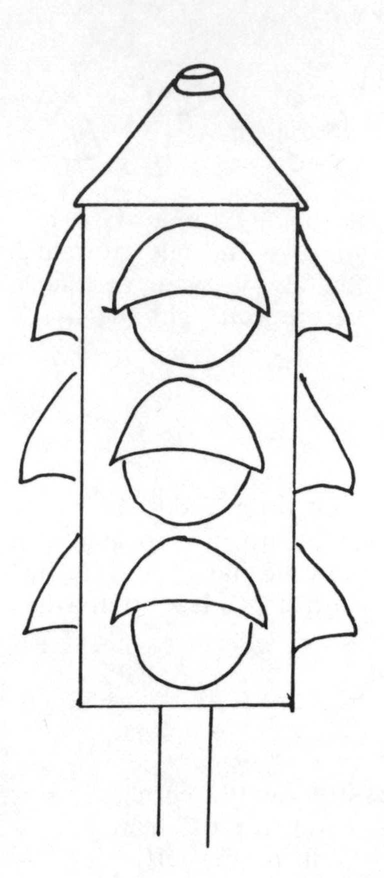

At the curb before I cross,
I stop my running feet. (Point to feet)
And look both ways to left and right
Before I cross the street.
Lest autos running quietly
Might come as a surprise.
I don't just listen with my ears, (Point to ears)
But look with both my eyes. (Point to eyes)

Traffic Lights

Do you know what traffic lights say to you?
Do you know what traffic lights say to do?
Yellow says, "Be careful" (Hold arm straight out)
Green says, "You may go." (Lower arm)
But red is most important, (Raise arm up)
It says, "Stop!" you know.

Soldiers and Sailors

Ten Little Soldiers

Ten little soldiers stand in a row (Both hands up, pointers extended)
They all bow down to the captain so! (Bend fingers down and up)
They march to the left, they march to the right. (Move hands to left and then to right)
They stand in a line all ready to fight! (Make two fists)
Then comes the captain with a great big gun. (Pointer fingers extended, thumbs up!)
Bang! went the gun and away they did run! (Clap hands, wiggle fingers and drop hands into lap)

Beat the Drum

Boom, boom, (Clap hands on each "Boom")
Beat the drum.
Boom, boom,
Here we come,
Boom, boom,
Do not lag.
Boom, boom,
Wave the flag. (Flag is four fingers on one hand held together, thumb resting on palm)

Attention

Attention, attention, Company A;
My fingers are playing soldier today; (Hold up ten fingers)
Attention, attention, Company B;
All salute, one, two, three; (Hand at forehead in salute)
The trumpets blow, too, too, too! (Hand at mouth)
My fingers march as soldiers do, (Motion of marching)
In a straight line, don't you see?
Company A and Company B,
Turn around; keep in step; (Move fingers left and right)
Off we go – hep, hep, hep! (Move hands behind back)
My finger soldiers every day
The general's commands always obey.

Marching

We are little soldiers,
Standing in a row; (Children stand)
Marching and saluting, (Children march time in place and salute)
Round and round we go; (Children march in small circles)
We are little soldiers,
Standing very tall; (Children continue marking time)
Turn about together,
Marching one and all! (Children turn in full circle)

Five Wooden Soldiers

Five wooden soldiers standing in a row; (Hold up five fingers)
Look out! Look out! Down they go!
Down goes little man, (Bend down little finger)
Down goes ring man, (Bend down ring finger)
Down goes middle man, (Bend down middle finger)
Down goes pointer, (Bend down pointer finger)
Down goes thumbkin; (Bend down thumb)
All five soldiers, lying just so!

Five Little Flags

Five little flags were waving in the breeze (One hand up)
And it's these five flags
That the wind likes to tease
For it tosses them up (Fingers flutter up)
And it tosses them down, (Fingers flutter down)
Before it decides
To move swiftly along. (Hand moves swiftly along)

Five Little Sailors

Five little sailors putting out to sea,
Rocking in their little boat, (Lace fingers and rock back and forth)
As happy as can be.
One is short and fat; (Hold up thumb)
The ship's cook is he;
Everyday he cooks the meals, one, two and three. (Pop up fingers)
One is the navigator, (Hold up pointer finger)
With a compass in his hand;
He tells about the weather, and he tells us where to land. (Hold up middle finger)
The bravest of them all; He gives us our directions and we hurry to his call.
The first mate is next in line, and then the cabin boy. (Ring, little finger)

Ten Little Sailors

Ten little sailors standing in a row: (Hold up ten fingers)
Ten little sailors salute just so, (Bend fingers)
They sail to the east: (Move fingers to left)
They sail to the west: (Move fingers to right)
Then back to the country they like best.
Where is this? Can you say? (Move fingers back to center)
Why, back to the good old U.S.A.! (Point to flag in room)

Ten Jolly Sailor Boys

Ten jolly sailor boys (Both hands up)
Dressed in blue.
Looking at me, (Turn hands towards face)
Looking at you. (Turn hands toward partner's face)

Transportation

Airplane

The airplane has great big wings; (Arms outstretched)
Its propeller spins around and sings. (Make one arm go)
"Vvvvvvv!"
The airplane goes up; (Lift arms)
The airplane goes down; (Lower arms)
The airplane flies high (Arms outstretched, turn body around)
Over our town!

Click–Clack

Click–Clack, Click–Clack (Place elbow on desk and swing arm)
Back and forth, forth and back
Wiper works with might and main
To keep the windshield free from rain.

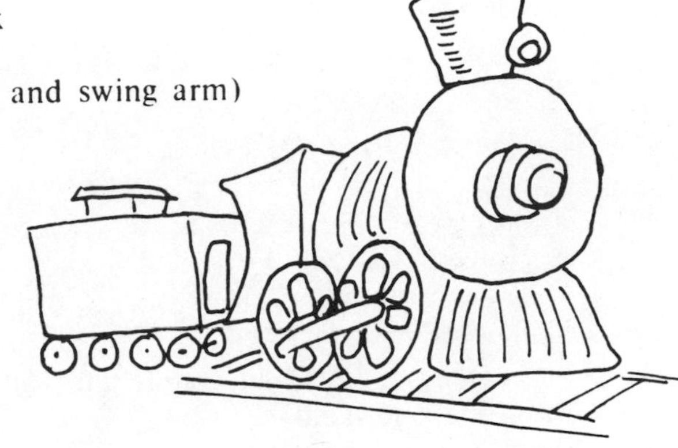

Engine

One is the engine, shiny and fine;
It pulls the coaches all in a line. (Hold up one finger)
Two is the baggage car, big and strong;
It carries suitcases and trunks along. (Hold up two fingers)
Three is the express car with double locks;
Send what you wish in a package or box. (Hold up three fingers)
Four is the mail car – red, white and blue;
It carries letters to me and you. (Hold up four fingers)
Five is the passenger car, so gay;
It carries people both night and day. (Hold up five fingers)
Six is the Pullman with berths one and two,
Where we can sleep the whole night through. (Hold up six fingers)
Seven is the dining car with tables so neat;
It's where I go when I want to eat. (Hold up seven fingers)
Eight is the observation car that gives a wide view;
It lets you see the countryside as you pass through. (Hold up eight fingers)
This is the train all ready to go
Through sunshine, wind, and rain, and snow.

Engine on the Track

Here is the engine on the track; (Hold up thumb)
Here is the coal car, just in back; (Hold up pointer)
Here is the box car to carry freight; (Hold up middle finger)
Here is the mail car. Don't be late! (Hold up ring finger)
Way back here at the end of the train (Hold up little finger)
Rides the caboose through the sun and the rain.

Riding in a Wagon

Riding in a wagon (Arms bend at elbows, forearms circling)
Riding in a wagon
Wheels go round and round and round
Riding in a wagon.

Counting

One, Two

One (Child stands and follows directions)
Show me one hand
Show me one finger
Wiggle one nose
Touch one arm
Shake one head
Sit one body down.

Two
Show me two hands
Wiggle two fingers
Shake two arms
Touch two eyes
Cover two ears
But sit one body down.

Two Little Dicky Birds

Two little dicky birds sitting on a wall (Fingers horizontal thumbs standing up)
One named Peter, the other named Paul. (Wiggle thumbs as named)
Fly away, Peter, fly away Paul. (Flutter hands behind back)
Come back Peter, come back Paul. (Bring hands back as before)

I See Three

I see three – one, two, three (Hold up three fingers, one at a time)
Three little bunnies
Reading the funnies (Hold hands open like pages)
I see three – one, two, three (Hold up three fingers as before)
Three kittens
Wearing mittens (Hold up fists)
I see three – one, two, three (Hold up three fingers again)
Three little frogs
Sitting on logs (Squat)
I see three – one, two, three (Hold up three fingers again)
Three little bears
Climbing upstairs (Pretend to climb)

Here Is a Ball

Here's a ball (Make circle with thumb and pointer)
And here's a ball (Make circle with two thumbs and pointers)
And a great big ball I see. (Make circle with arms)
Now let's count the balls we've made,
One, two, three. (Repeat as above)

Little Pussies

One, two, three, four. (Hold up four fingers of left hand, touch each one.)
One, two, three, four.
These little pussies came to my door.
They just stood there (Fingers straight)
And said, "Good-day". (Bend fingers together)
And then they tiptoed away. (Move fingers behind back)

Ready for School

Two little houses closed up tight (Fists closed up thumbs in)
Open up the windows and let in the light (Fingers open)
Ten little finger people tall and straight (Palms to front, fingers erect)
Ready for school at half past eight. (Fingers erect, hands and arms move forward)

Five Little Birds

Five little birds without any home (Hold up five fingers)
Five little trees in a row (Raise hands high over head)
Come build your nest in our branches tall (Cup hands)
We'll rock them to and fro. (Rock nest)

Five Little Seashells

Five little seashells lying on the shore; (Hold up five fingers)
Swish! went the waves, and then there were four. (Bend down one finger)
Four little seashells, cozy as could be;
Swish! went the waves, and then there were three. (Bend down one finger)
Three little seashells all pearly new;
Swish! went the waves, and then there were two. (Bend down one finger)
Two little seashells sleeping in the sun;
Swish! went the waves, and then there was one. (Bend down one finger)
One little seashell left all alone
Whispered "Shhhhhhhhhhhh" as I took it home. (Bend down last finger)

Five Little Letters

Five little letters lying on a tray. (Five fingers up)
Mommy came in and took the first away. (Thumb down)
Then Daddy said, "The big one is for me." (Pointer down)
I counted them again and then there were three. (Count)
Big brother Bill asked, "Did I get any mail?"
He found one and cried, "A letter from Gale." (Middle finger down)
My sister Jane took the next to last,
And ran upstairs to open it fast. (Ring finger down)
I wonder for whom the last one will be.
I can't read but I hope it's for me. (Wiggle little finger)

The Zoo

One, one, the zoo is lots of fun (Hold up one finger in each hand)
Two, two, see a kangaroo (Hold up two fingers in each hand)
Three, three, see a chimpanzee (Three fingers, each hand)
Four, four, hear the lions roar. (Four fingers, each hand)
Five, five, watch the seals dive. (Five fingers, each hand)

Ten Little Fingers

I have ten little fingers and ten little toes. (Children point to portions of body as they repeat words)
Two little arms and one little nose,
One little mouth and two little ears.
Two little eyes for smiles and tears,
One little head and two little feet.
One little chin, that's (Child's name) complete.

Me

I have five fingers on each hand. (Point to each body part as it is named)
Ten toes on both feet;
Two ears, two eyes, one nose, one mouth
With which to gently speak.
My hands can clap.
My feet can tap.
My eyes can brightly shine.
My ears can hear.
My nose can smell.
My mouth can make a rhyme.

Captain and His Men

One, two, three, four, five in a row, (Pop up fingers one at a time on right hand)
A captain and his men!
And on the other side, you know,
Are six, seven, eight, nine, ten (Pop up fingers one at a time on left hand)

Ten Little Indians

One little, two little, three little Indians, (Three fingers up)
Four little, five little, six little Indians, (Three more go up)
Seven little, eight little, nine little Indians, (Three more go up)
Ten little Indian boys. (Or maidens)

Learn to Count

One, two, three and four;
I can count even more.
Five, six, seven, eight;
See my fingers standing straight. (Raise one finger at a time as you count)
Nine and ten are my thumb men. (Raise thumbs)

Ten Little Ducklings

Ten little ducklings, (Move hands back and forth in waddling motion)
Dash, dash, dash!
Jumped in the duck pond (Motion of jumping)
Splash, splash, splash!
When the mother called them,
"Quack, quack, quack"
Ten little ducklings
Swam right back. (Motion of swimming)

Nursery Rhymes

Jack and Jill

Jack and Jill went up the hill (Motion of two fingers climbing up an arm)
To fetch a pail of water.
Jack fell down (One finger doubled under)
And broke his crown,
And Jill came tumbling after. (Both fingers doubled under)

Little Miss Muffet

Little Miss Muffet sat on a tuffet (Fist with thumb standing)
Eating her curds and whey. (Pretend to eat)
Along came a spider (Running motion with fingers)
And sat down beside her, ("Spider" sits down beside "tuffet")
And frightened Miss Muffet away. (Throw hands out)

Little Jack Horner

Little Jack Horner
Sat in the corner,
Eating his Christmas pie. (Pretend to eat from pie)
He put in his thumb (Put thumb in pie)
And pulled out a plum, (Pull it out)
And said, "What a good boy am I." (Hold thumb up)

Little Bo-Peep

Little Bo-Peep has lost her sheep, (Hold up both hands with fingers extended)
And can't tell where to find them (Hide hands behind back)
Leave them alone and they'll come home, (Bring hands from behind back and hold them up)
Wagging their tails behind them (Wiggle fingers)

Hickory Dickory Dock

Hickory Dickory Dock (Raise right arm high)
The mouse ran up the clock. (Run fingers of left hand up right arm)
The clock struck one. (Clap hands over head)
The mouse ran down. (Run fingers down arm)
Hickory Dickory Dock.

Jack Be Nimble

Jack be nimble, (Hold closed fist with thumb standing)
Jack be quick,
Jack jump over (First hand hops over second)
the candlestick.

Two Black Birds

There were two blackbirds
Sitting on a hill, (Hold up both hands, thumbs erect, fingers bent)
The one named Jack, (Wiggle one thumb)
The other named Jill (Wiggle other thumb)
Fly away, Jack! (Bend down one thumb)
Fly away, Jill! (Bend down other thumb)
Come back, Jack! (Raise one thumb erect)
Come back, Jill! (Raise other thumb erect)

Here Sits the Lord Mayor

Here sits the Lord Mayor, (Point to forehead)
Here sit his two men; (Point to eyes)
Here sits a rooster, (Point to right cheek)
And here sits a hen. (Point to left cheek)
Here sit the chickens (Point to nose)
Here they run in; (Point to mouth)
Chin-chopper, chin-chopper, (Move chin up and down with fingers)
Chin-chopper, chin!

Pat A Cake

Pat a cake, pat a cake, baker's man! (Clap four times in rhythm)
Bake me a cake as fast as you can. (Cup hands)
Pat it, and dot it and mark it with B, (Pantomine this action)
And put it in the oven (Extend both hands)
For Baby and me. (Point to member of class and then to self)

Little Boy Blue

Little Boy Blue, come blow your horn; (Hold up clenched hands in a make believe horn)
The sheep are in the meadow, (Hold up left hand and bend down fingers)
The cows are in the corn (Hold up right hand and bend down fingers)
Where is the little boy who looks after the sheep? (Spread hands questioningly)
He's under the haystack,
Fast asleep! (Place palms together and lay head to one side on hands)

Sing a Song of Sixpence

Sing a song of sixpence,
A pocket full of rye; (Place hands in imaginary pockets)
Four-and-twenty blackbirds (Flap arms)
Baked in a pie. (Make circle with arms)
When the pie was opened,
The birds began to sing! (Two or three children whistle)
Wasn't that a dainty dish
To set before the king?

The king was in his counting house,
Counting out his money. (Motion of piling coins on top of each other)
The queen was in the parlor,
Eating bread and honey (Motion of eating)
The maid was in the garden,
Hanging up the clothes.
When down came a blackbird (Flap arms)
And snipped off her nose. (Pinch nose)

Activity Verses

Little Bear

Little Bear, Little Bear, turn around (Turn around)
Little Bear, Little Bear, touch the ground (Touch the floor)
Little Bear, Little Bear, climb the stairs (Pretend to climb stairs)
Little Bear, Little Bear, say your prayers (Fold hands)
Little Bear, Little Bear, turn out the light (Pretend to turn off light)
Little Bear, Little Bear, say "Good-night." (Lay head to side on hands)

Merry-Go-Round

Ride with me on the merry-go-round,
Around and around and around; (Move one hand in circles)
Up go the horses, up! (Raise arms in the air)
Down go the horses, down! (Lower arms)
You ride a horse that is white; (Point to neighbor)
I ride a horse that is brown; (Point to self)
Up and down on the merry-go-round, (Raise and lower arms; then move one hand in circles)
Our horses go round and round.

Pop! Pop! Pop!

Pop! Pop! Pop! (Clap hands)
Pour the corn into the pot.
Pop! Pop! Pop! (Clap hands)
Take and shake it 'til it's hot.
Pop! Pop! Pop! (Clap hands)
Lift the lid – what have we got?
Pop! Pop! Pop! (Clap hands)
POPCORN! (Say loudly)

Popcorn

Sing a song of popcorn
When the snowstorms rage;
Fifty little brown men
Put into a cage. (Cup hands together, palms in, fingertips touching)
Shake them all – they laugh and leap (Shake cage)
Crowding to the top.
Watch them burst their little coats
Pop! Pop! Pop! (Clap three times)

House

This is the roof of the house so good (Make peaked roof with hands)
These are the walls that are made of wood, (Hands straight, palms parallel)
These are the windows that let in the light, (Thumbs and pointer finger form window)
This is the door that shuts so tight, (Hands straight side by side)
This is the chimney so straight and tall, (Arm up straight)
Oh, what a good house for one and all. (Arms at angle for roof)

The Teapot

I'm a little teapot, short and stout
This is my handle (Put one hand on hip)
This is my spout. (Extend opposite arm sideways, hand out)
When I get all steamed up, then I shout
Just tip me over and pour me out. (Bend body toward extended arm)
I'm a very clever pot, it's true.
Here's an example of what I can do.
I can change my handle and change my spout (Change position of hands)
Just tip me over and pour me out. (Bend body in opposite direction)

Choo-Choo Train

This is a choo-choo train (Bend arms at elbows)
Puffing down the track. (Rotate forearms in rhythm)
Now it's going forward, (Push arms forward; continue rotating motion)
Now the bell is ringing. (Pull bell cord with closed fist)
Now the whistle blows. (Hold fist near mouth and blow)
What a lot of noise it makes. (Cover ears with hands)
Everywhere it goes.

Wooden William

I'm just like Wooden William
Who stands up straight and tall. (Stand stiff and straight)
My arms and legs are wooden (Arms hang rigidly at sides)
They just don't move at all.

Zig-Zag Children

I know a little zig-zag boy
Who goes this way and that (Two steps to left, two steps to right)
He never knows just where he puts
His coat or shoes or hat. (Point to shoulders, shoes, head)

I know a little zig-zag girl,
Who flutters here and there (Hands flutter to left and right)
She never knows just where to find
Her brush to fix her hair. (Point to hair)

If you are not a zig-zag child,
You'll have no cause to say
That you forgot, for you will know
Where things are put away.

Sometimes My Hands Are Naughty

Sometimes my hands are naughty (Slap hand)
And so my mother says
That she will have to scold them,
And send them off to bed. (Close eyes, lay head on hands)
So little hands be careful, please, (Look down at hands)
Of everything you do.
Because if you are sent to bed,
I'll have to go there, too.

Draw a Circle

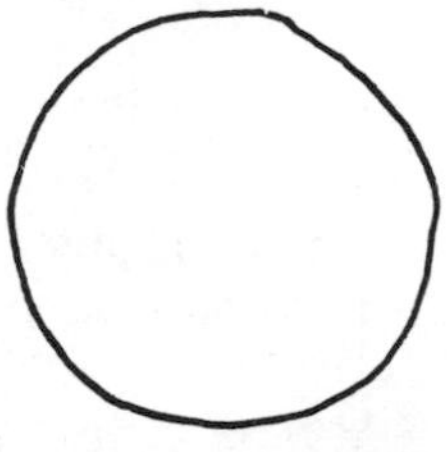

Draw a circle, draw a circle (Draw circles in the air with finger)
Round as can be
Draw a circle, draw a circle
Just for me. (Draw circles in the air with finger)

Draw a square, draw a square (Draw a square in the air)
Shaped like a box
Draw a square, draw a square
With corners four.

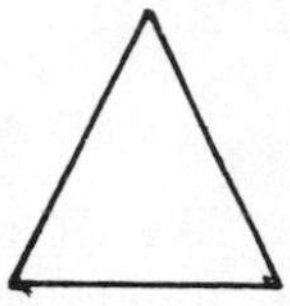

Draw a triangle, draw a triangle (Draw a triangle in the air)
With corners three.
Draw a triangle, draw a triangle
Just for me.

Washing Clothes

Here is a little washboard, (Slant one hand down)
And here is a little tub. (Bring thumbs and fingertips of hands together)
Here is a little cake of soap, (Thumb and fingertips of one hand together)
And this is how we rub.
Here is the clothesline way up high (Hold arms straight up, hands clenched)
Where the clothes are drying,
Here the wind comes oo–oo–oo
Now the clothes are drying.

This Baby Pig

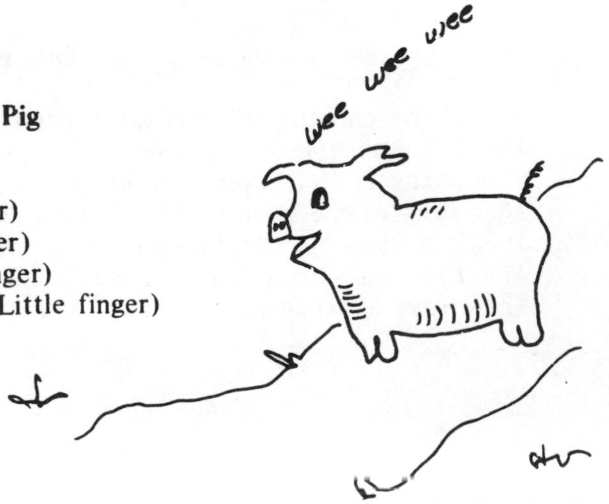

This baby pig went to market; (Thumb)
This baby pig trimmed the tree; (Pointer finger)
This baby pig cooked the dinner, (Middle finger)
And this baby pig sang, "Wee, wee." (Ring finger)
And this baby pig cried, "Merry Christmas." (Little finger)
To everyone he did see.

wee wee wee

Hammer, Hammer, Hammer

Hammer, hammer, hammer, (Pound fist on other palm)
I drive the nails so straight.
Do you know what I'm building?
A truck for hauling freight.
I'm sawing, sawing, sawing (Move hand back and forth on opposite palm)
To make my wheels go round;
I nail my truck together,
Pound, pound, pound. (Pound fist on opposite palm)

Floppy Rag Doll

I'm a floppy, floppy rag doll, (Sit with head, arms and shoulders drooping)
Drooping in my chair, (Continue relaxed position, head, arms and shoulders drooping, hips well back against chair)
My head just rolls from side to side, (Roll head over to left shoulder then slowly roll it around to fall limply over right shoulder)
My arms fall through the air. (Still sitting, let hands hang completely relaxed, over side of chair, and swing very slowly in limp fashion, from shoulder sockets)

Flopsy Flora

I'm just like Flopsy Flora
My doll that's made of rags.
My arms go flop – my feet go plop (Flop arms at sides, flop feet up and down)
My head just wigs and wags. (Move head drom side to side)

Baby

Here is baby's tousled head (Make a fist)
He nods and nods; (Bend fist back and forth)
Let's put him to bed. (Bend other arm and tuck fist into crook of elbow)

This is the Church

This is the church (Fingers interlocked, palms together)
This is the steeple (Two pointer fingers up to form steeple)
This is the bell (Fingers interlocked and palms together)
That calls to the people. (Rock hands back and forth like pealing bell)
This is a chair (Right fingertips bent and touching left palm)
And this is a piano (Move fingers as if playing piano)
That plays a sweet air.

Time To Go To Bed

Climbing, climbing up the stairs, (Pretend to climb stairs)
It's time to go to bed (Place head on folded hands)
I'll thump my fluffy pillow,
Fold back my mother's spread. (Pretend to fold back spread)
I'll brush my teeth and wash my hands. (Pretend to brush teeth and wash hands)
Turn out my bedside light,
And whisper as I tuck in bed.
"God keep me through the night." (Place head on folded hands)

Going to Bed

This little boy (girl) is going to bed (Lay pointer in palm)
Down on the pillow he lays his head (Thumb acts as pillow)
Covers himself with the blankets so tight (Wrap fingers around "boy")
And this is the way he sleeps all night. (Close eyes)
Morning comes, and he opens his eyes. (Open eyes)
Throws back the covers, and up he flies. (Open fingers)
Soon he is up and dressed and away. (Pointer stands straight)
Ready for school and ready for play.

Jack-In-The-Box

Jack-in-the-box all shut up tight. (Fingers wrapped around thumb)
Not a breath of air, not a ray of light. (Other hand covers first)
How tired you must be all down in a heap. (Lift off)
I'll open the lid and up you will leap. (Thumb pops up)

I Can Make a Hammock

I can make a hammock. (Lock fingers, palms up)
I can make a cup. (Cup hands)
Here's the way to make a ball (Fingers and thumbs touch for circle)
Here's how I toss it up! (Tossing motion)

1541